Between the Heart and the Land/
Entre el corazón y la tierra

Latina Poets
in the Midwest

Brenda Cárdenas
Johanny Vázquez Paz
Editors

The Nepantla Latin@
Collection

"Between Two Worlds"

100% Title V Grant Funded

MARCH/Abrazo books are available at special discounts in bulk purchases for sales, promotions or premiums. For more information, contact:
Small Press Distribution
1341 Seventh Street, Berkeley, CA 94710-1409
Ph: 510-524-1668 Fax: 510-524-0852

Library of Congress Cataloging-in-Publication Data
Between the Heart and the Land / Entre el corazón y la tierra:
Latina Poets in the Midwest /
Brenda Cárdenas and Johanny Vázquez Paz, editors
Includes biographical references.

ISBN 1-877636-18-5 (pbk)
1. American literature—U.S. Latina poets. 2. U.S. Latina women—Literary collections. 3. U.S. Latinos—Literary collections. 4. American literature—Women poets. 5. American literature—Midwest poets. 6. English/Spanish Poetry.
I. Cárdenas, Brenda, 1961- . II. Vázquez Paz, Johanny, 1960- .

Library of Congress Catalogue Card Number #00 093690.

Cover art: *Dream I* by María Dolores Mercado, 2000.
Cover graphic design by Bohemian Communications.
Photography by Mayra Morris and Pete Rodríguez.

Printed and bound in U.S.A.

First Edition, 2001
6 5 4 3 2 1

Published by El Movimiento Artístico Chicano MARCH, Inc.
MARCH/Abrazo Press, P.O. Box 2890, Chicago, IL 60690

This project is funded by the people of Aztlán.

*To all the Latinas
living between coasts and cultures:
May their voices be heard.*

Brenda Cárdenas would like to thank her entire family, especially her parents José and Diane Cárdenas; her "second" parents Elia and Karel Kotnik; her mentor Maurice Kilwein Guevara; and her friends who have been collaborators, commiserators, editors, and supporters of her work: Janet, Reneé, Jefe, Alejandra, Jason, Eli B., Michele, Anthony, Johanny, Frances, Brian Komei, Gina, Milton, Yolanda, MariCarmen, JAM, Evelina, Regine, Jeanne, the Sonido Ink(quieto) crew—José, Juan, Ricardo, Jesús, and Aidé—; Eleazar, Silvia and the gente at the Café Jumping Bean; Julie, Mario and the Guild Complex; Nina and Word Gourmet; and the many students she has worked with over the years with a special shout out to Anna Z.

Johanny Vázquez Paz would like to thank Thelma Paz; Vivian Vázquez; María Vázquez; Brandon Tilton; Wilfredo Nieves; Brenda Cárdenas for the translations and true friendship; José Osvaldo; Freddie, Pipo, Haydeé, Oscar, Raúl, Tadeo—all fans of my poetry in Puerto Rico—; Martín, Rosario, Lito and Sonia—big supporters in Chicago—; and Antonio Vázquez and Griselle Vázquez, who gave me so much in life and whom I still miss dearly.

Contents

Foreword
By Frances R. Aparicio

Between the Heart and the Land is a most appropriate title for this rich and much-awaited collection of poetry by Latinas in the Midwest. If the heart and the land are suggested here as opposites, it is because this sample of poems, like all poetry, articulates the dialectics between immanence and transcendence, between the spiritual realm and our material being and physicality. At another level, the title is a linguistic pun on the Midwest as the heartland of the United States. While this region may be considered as the center of life in the popular imagination of Anglo-America, in the context of Latino/a Studies it remains understudied and underrepresented in most scholarship produced on the West and East Coasts. While the literary voices of U.S. Puerto Rican poets and fiction writers on the East Coast and of their Chicano/a counterparts on the West Coast and in the Southwest have been anthologized, duly canonized and even mainstreamed by the Anglo literary market, very little is heard about Latino/a writers and poets in the Midwest. This is ironic, partly because renowned writers such as Sandra Cisneros, Ana Castillo, and Cuban-American Achy Obejas either grew up, have lived or currently live in Chicago. In addition, *The Americas Review*, the principal journal of U.S. Latino/a literature, emerged in the 1970s as Revista Chicano-Riqueña in Gary, Indiana. Thus, the history of Latino/a literary production in the Midwest and the ways in which this region, both as an urban center and as rural, agricultural communities, informs and contextualizes these voices is a topic that waits to be examined.

This anthology, edited by two important Latina poets in the Chicago area, Brenda Cárdenas and Johanny Vázquez Paz, and published by March/Abrazo Press, represents various significant stances. First, this co-editorship reflects the collaboration between a Mexican-American and a Puerto Rican, an interlatina leadership and effort that is most historically characteristic of the Midwest. Published by a Latino press rather than by a New York mainstream publishing house, this anthology also suggestively contests the unilateral mainstreaming of Latino/a literary voices by the New York literary market that has rampantly co-opted the oppositional writers among us. The decision to publish in a bilingual format and, moreover, to publish not only Spanish translations or English versions of the Spanish, but interlingual poems and poems with different versions in each language, likewise contests the English-Only tendencies of Latina literature in the mainstream market. All of these elements constitute a reclaiming of decision-making and of authority in the selection, representation, and dissemination of our literary production.

Glancing through the biographies of the contributors, it is clear that the definition of a "Latina" poet at this historical juncture is not exclusively that of working-class Chicanas or Puerto Rican militant feminists. Rather, it encompasses a rich array of women of various national Origins—Dominicans, Colombians, Argentinians, Cubans, Costa Ricans, Bolivians, Salvadorans, Mexicans, Chicanas, Puerto Ricans—as well as of diverse socioeconomic and work experiences, sexuality and sexual identities, ages and generational experiences, and urban/rural contexts. From performance artists and professors to entrepreneurs, community leaders and educators, the women who speak here articulate, in a most varied array of styles, textures, and voicings, their gendered and racialized subjectivities as minorities in the United States. Migration and the border, hybridity and biculturalism, language and identity, erotic desire and lesbian identities, marriage, the pain of abandonment by lovers and fathers, politics and the subordination of our communities, and the struggles to survive as modern women in an urban metropolis without denying the positive traditions of our cultures are reflected about in poems that move us emotionally and are intellectually powerful at the same time. It is worthy of attention to foreground the very "universal" subtexts and influences that inform many of these works, echoes that reveal the very heterogeneous social locations of Latina poets in the Midwest. Echoes of Pablo Neruda, Alfonsina Storni, Alurista, Walt Whitman, Julio

Cortázar, Carlos Fuentes, Ulysses, Dyonisius and Yemayá, Rubén Blades, Federico García Lorca, and Juan Luis Guerra, the shadows of the Holocaust, and the abuelitas—those working women who have served as pillars and models of strength and resistance to the younger generations but who are invisible to history—resonate throughout these pages. To say, then, that this is only a local anthology, or a regional project, would not pay justice to the multiple sets of knowledge and axes of reference that define the poetic production of these women. I am honored to have been invited to open this unique and significant anthology, one that reminds readers that the Midwest constitutes an important and active space for Latina literary creativity. Muchas gracias to Brenda and Johanny for making this possible!

Introduction

Over the past fifteen years we have welcomed the gradual proliferation of Latino/a literary anthologies that are edited by some of the country's foremost writers, poets and scholars, such as Miguel Algarín; Martín Espada; Roberta Fernández; Ray González; Bryce Milligan, Mary Guerrero Milligan and Angela de Hoyos; and Tey Diana Rebolledo and Eliana S. Rivero, among others. Such anthologies have been fundamental in granting visibility to U.S. Latina/o poetry and in assisting both emerging and established poets to further advance their vocations. These collections have been valuable resources from which we have learned, taught, and received inspiration. In addition, many of the editors have gone to great lengths to ensure the representation of culturally and aesthetically diverse voices. Most collections include at least a few younger poets first embarking on their careers. Some are even dedicated solely to the work of Latina women. However, aside from a few incredibly gifted and very famous Latina writers who grew up and began their careers in the Midwest, most of the Latinas published repeatedly have been from the East and West Coasts or the Southwest.

We applaud this body of literature. Yet as poets who have been living, writing, performing and teaching in the Midwest for many years, we have keenly felt the absence of literature by Midwestern Latinas in anthologies and magazines and on the shelves of bookstores and libraries. We have encountered countless Latina poets who are quite active within the literary communities of the nation's heartland. Their names may be recognized by audiences in Chicago, Milwaukee, Detroit or Minneapolis, and they may be quite persistent in seeking publication, on occasion with success, but they are also often marginalized both outside of and within the national Latina/o literary scene. Such limited visibility is common despite the fact that, according to Robert Aponte's and Marcelo E. Siles' 1997 report, there are approximately 60,000,000 Latinos/as living in the Midwest.

We are indebted to our predecessors who have edited and published anthologies of Midwestern Latina/o poetry. Among them are *Nosotros: A Collection of Latino Poetry and Graphics from Chicago* (*Revista Chicano-Riqueña*, 1977); Oscar Mireles' *I Didn't Know There Were Latinos in Wisconsin I* (1989) and *II* (1999); Carlos Cumpián's *Emergency Tacos*, a collection of Chicago Latina/o poets (MARCH/Abrazo Press, 1989); and Olivia Maciel's *Astillas de Luz / Shards of Light,* a richly bilingual anthology of Chicago Latina/o poets (Tía Chucha Press, 1998).

Between the Heart and the Land / Entre el corazón y la tierra follows in this tradition but also builds on it. Rather than focusing on poets from a particular city or state, we have chosen to emphasize poetry by Latina women from throughout the Midwest. In doing so, we hope to expose readers to the incredible diversity and excellent work of Latina poets who are writing at the nation's center—between cultures, languages and coasts. We also want to create a space in and from which these poets might dialogue with one another. In keeping with our Midwestern focus, we selected cover art by Dolores Mercado, a Mexican visual artist and educator living in Chicago. We then asked Bohemian Communications—a cutting-edge graphic design firm in Chicago that is owned and operated by three young Latino entrepreneurs—to design the book's cover. It is also important that Chicago's MARCH/Abrazo Press initiated and funded this project, especially in light of the fact that it has been publishing the work of Latina/o and Native American poets and writers, most of whom have been Midwesterners, for the past fifteen years.

To create this anthology, we solicited submissions from the many Midwestern *poetas* whom we have known, known about, or whose work we have read. We also sent a call for submissions to literary organizations, universities, colleges, cultural and community institutions, and independent bookstores throughout the Midwest. We received a large response from some cities and states but, unfortunately, no response from others. Furthermore, some poets whose work we solicited decided not to submit.

As Frances Aparicio points out in her foreword, a

main goal of this book is to highlight a large cross section of Midwestern Latina poets. Some of the poets we have included have published in literary magazines and other anthologies. A few have their own chapbooks or full-length collections. And some are being published here for the first time. Those gathered here represent many heritages with origins in Mexico, Central America, the Caribbean and South America. Some of these writers were born in the Midwest, and all of them currently live in Indiana, Illinois, Minnesota, and Wisconsin. Within these pages, you will find poems that incorporate readily identifiable cultural symbols and signifiers, as well as those that bear few traces of particular ethnic origins. You will read pieces specifically situated in the Midwest as well as those that are situated in other landscapes and broader contexts. You will encounter lyric, narrative, performance and formalist poems as well as interlingual and monolingual poems in either English or Spanish.

Overall, by representing as many voices, styles, and aesthetics as possible, we have tried to present the breadth and depth of the emerging tradition of Midwestern Latina poetry. Furthermore, we hope that *Between the Heart and the Land* will lead to wider inclusion of such poetry in future anthologies. Even greater is our hope for the release of more individual full-length collections by the many talented Midwestern Latina poets writing today.

Our deepest thanks to all the poets for their patience through this long process; to Carlos Cumpián, Cynthia Gallaher, and all MARCH members for the opportunity; to Frances Aparicio for her thoughtful foreword and incredible support; to Brian Komei Dempster for providing feedback on our Introduction; to Dolores Mercado for her artistic vision; and to everyone at Bohemian Communications for their generous donation of time and creativity. Finally, much respect and gratitude to the established Midwestern Latina poets and writers, Ana Castillo, Sandra Cisneros and Achy Obejas, for paving the way.

Brenda Cárdenas and Johanny Vázquez Paz
March, 2001

Denia M. Alvarado

Am I Me?

I come from a place
green and lush
made warm and fragrant
by breathing winds,

a place where quick hands loosen the smell of maize
with the rush of a river stone
and the heat of an iron grate.
My inaudible jungle lives in Eden's hush
where fear of rain forest consumption rushes
the pseudo men to flush
the rest away.

My roots, transplanted
from tropical garden
to concrete jungle,
live in fear of a cold,
dark world of frosty orchids.

In the midst of a blizzard
when the sun has long been hidden
from my cacao skin turned
the color of moist masa,
I must ask, am I me?

Most times, the price we pay is high
for being hybrid flowers
not truly of this land,
through time, not wholly
of the other.

I speak words of a strange language.
My mind straddles concepts
absent from my native culture.

Nuestro lenguaje tiene doble filo;
uno nos une, el otro nos corta.
Speak English!
A veces, con suerte
nos piden que hablemos
nuestra lengua melodiosa
romántica y afable.

Y en esos instantes les digo
con gusto acepto
mi parte en ser Latina
Americana.

En esta Rica Costa
No estamos en Costa Rica

I
En mi tierra negra
lanza como pantera
de hierro
el dolor de la pansa vacía.
En esta tierra,
hoy llena,
no es ella
sino el alma
que llora
en su soledad y vacío,
en su falta de sol
y caricias del viento Caribeño.

In my black soil
the pang of hunger strikes
swiftly as the panther's deadly lunge!
Appetite has brought me here—
to this lush yellow of gold and wheat.
Today, the belly full,
another pain assails from a place within—
a hollow cave where memories are
the jagged edges on walls of petrified soil.
My soul craves an intangible—
an afternoon lying in a hammock
swinging in the gentle warmth
of the Caribbean flow—
the smell of refried beans wrapped in banana leaves,
the sound of tropical rains
on corrugated aluminum canopies.
My belly full, my soul cries
empty.

II
If no art is found
in a child's world,
what tool is used to measure beauty?
If no poem describes her world,
what metaphor tells her story?
If no art is found
in a child's world,
where do her aesthetic tears flow?

III
This blooming in my mind
is watered by words flowing in my ears,
views that nourish becomings
which may never be or come.
Imagination is
living possibilities that strive to survive
inside the walls of fingers that can't feel,
lips that can't kiss,
warm breath that can't exhale.
Existing,
we hunger to love the inner soul
but are blocked by barriers
that measure imperfections of time.
We yearn
for yesterday's land
of blue sapphire rivers and green
emerald forests made of rain—
an enchanted world that breast-fed
banana nectar to fluorescent hummingbirds
and aquamarine to heaven.

Reflections

after Jon Crane's Heartland Reflections, *1992*

This house with its lackluster color mocks me.
Its windows reproach me.
I'm fenced-in by the facade
of our landscaped lives.
My husband, I am the land-locked water
that reflects your image drifting.

This morning what is imprisoned
threatens to escape.
Every breath of this green I fell in love with
conquers any hope for the orange-red of day.

I walk from room to room
by the hand of white silence.
Remember the children? Strangers.
I see strangers in the faces
I gave birth to.

But I am the stranger,
the slave trader.
I sold out
for the tender shoots outside,
glad that someone paid for a gold band
to appropriate my pink world.

Morning is gone.
Reflections beckon
in borderless waters.
Our passions could be unleashed there—
the only place we dare to touch.

Beatriz Badikian-Gartler

Neither Here nor There

Neither here nor there I stand, one foot
on this side of the border, one on the other. Were
I to have three more feet, I'd easily place them on
three more lands. Neither here nor there, where
am I? And people say: you are everywhere, multiple,
you are fortunate. I respond: "many" carries
the danger of becoming "none." Invisible I stand.

I Have Been Painting on Leaves

I have been painting on leaves.
Between waxed sheets of paper they sleep
when I'm not working on them.
Like looking at the gorillas in the zoo
behind their glass cages. Like the "boli"
in the Art Institute: mud, stick, blood,
and bone. "The pot is the thing that
bridges, joins together," says Heidegger, and
I begin to make vessels. Clay enters through
hand and eye, I enter the clay: we breathe in,
take a drink from each other. Body and
clay remember, touch, measure, and
record. Wisdom of the body.

Our Work

Our work is so different! You paint
bottles and stools, abstract garbage cans,
an explosion of black on yellow, blue on red,
fish, leaves, an American flag, the sun

me?

one crazy lizard: red-green-yellow with blue
in the background, one small eye on the top,
one big eye all the way down. Rectangles
dialogue with circles, squares interrupt diamonds,
lines crisscross up and down, undulating. I like
the bright primaries, the scary greens and ominous
purples. You prefer white surfaces, clean black
lines, an orange in gray, an insect I don't recognize.

I paint my history in red and black, fill in
the blanks with pain and mourning, a melancholy-blue
sky,
a single word.

Cajas de zapatos

La tierra lava y plancha entre
mis dedos, con almidón
y agua, para que quede lindo. Los libros
nadan felices y tranquilos
como truchas
hacia el mar.
Mi madre le pone fuego a mis zapatos
y las cajas estornudan y escupen, me tosen en la cara.
Las sostengo con cuidado, meticulosamente,
en las palmas de mis manos. Cajas llenas de
aire y de agua—¿es ésto lo que Pandora tenía
en mente cuando las regalaba? Cajas
de zapatos
útiles para guardar cosas: aire, agua, fuego, tierra.

ᄿ ᄿ ᄿ

Shoeboxes

Between my toes, the earth sews
and irons, sprinkling starch
and water daintily. The books
swim happily like trout
upstream.
My mother sets fires
in my shoes. The boxes sneeze
when I look at them. Coughing
and spitting, blowing their noses, and
spitting some more. I hold them carefully in the palms
of my hands and walk on air, on water. Little boxes
with fire—is this what Pandora had in mind when
she gave them away?
Shoeboxes
good for saving things:
air, fire, water, earth.

Sonia Báez-Hernández

Container

I can listen to sadness
taking over my body.

I can eat my tears
in mutating silence.

I can touch the light of
the candle—de la vela—
that penetrates my left
nipple—mi pesón,

a container of rosarios.

My skin is a container,
un rosario de espasmos—
my skin in transmutation of
agonies.

I can listen to sadness
taking over my body.

I can eat my tears
in mutating silence.

There Is Something

In the middle of the night
I walk
con piedras
between my legs.

In the middle of the night
I walk with desire
between my
legs.

In the middle of desire
I walk with the night
between my legs.

In the middle of the night
I walk with ashes
between my legs.

In the middle of the night
I walk with a triangle
between my legs.

In the middle of the night
I walk
with a death-desire
between my legs.

Brenda Cárdenas

from Spanish Sound Waves (a series)

"The river on the other side / of English is carrying the message."
—Víctor Hernández Cruz

Duración—V

> *Aquí vuelan aves arracimadas como uvas*
Clusters perch over
open-mouthed stones.
These sculpted men arc back,
necks straining toward gods and vines,
elbows raised in angles.
Birds veil the starved sun.

> *Aquí vuelan aves arracimadas*
This is the *V* in Cabeza de Vaca
sweating the salt of the bay
in a migration that halts and hovers.
Is it the glint of obsidian that lures
vultures to the eye of earth?
Or jade of stone beasts that pull
thieves up the open-legged vertices
of our pyramids? We vanish

> *Aquí vuelan aves*
in the wind worn skull of the long-
horn, in mutations making bowls
of eye sockets, cups of its keratin.
We carve hilts for our bowies
from the open jaw. We feed.
Muscle is a buzzard's feast,
our brazos his power to swarm.

> *Aquí*
The new sounds echo
a chamber older than memory.

Our *V's* fling their arms open
and come back to us. *B's.*
We have seen balas
faster than veins of light
etching the night sky.

They fill our heads with ringing.

Intensidad—Ñ

El campesino rolls
his shoulder blades as he turns
from the furrows toward
the road's curve home,
Otro año, otro día, otra estación;
le ha añejado con su añojal.

~Ñ, the yawn in mañana~

La araña weaves her web of music,
tuning its strings while she sings
de sus compañeras obrando
en las cabañas, labrando
en los campos de caña.
She holds the high notes,
pulling filaments taut.
And when a fly's wing
touches one fiber,
everything vibrates.

~la añagaza del balance~

A cat's arch and curled spine
stretches into the long afternoon.
Sueña con alimañas
espiando en las montañas;
sueña con carne,

the wiry tension
of spring and pounce
on the small-boned
and the broken-winged.

~ the sneer of engaño~

Deep heat of day rises
like a serpent from its cool tomb
entrañado beneath the sand,
leaves its tilde trace, la señal
that loosens and fades,
one moment sliding
into centuries of terrain.

~el diseño antiguo del futuro~

Diamond-skinned Kukulcán,
guiñando desde el cielo,
slides past clouds over the edge
of sun at the tip of Chichén
onto a shadow of stone,
the equinox of a plumed past.

~the slow and brilliant tilt de los añosos~

Coiled in mantillas pañosas
y la rumble of street noise,
the fire-eater waits for night
to define the sharp outlines
of sustenance—
su extrañeza y su ceño,
sus llantos oscuros de daño—
eyes squeezed tight
above the blackened rim
of his open mouth.

~Ñ, the grimace of resistance~
~La ñacanima y la luz~

Report from the Temple of Confessions in Old Chicano English

—after an installation by Guillermo Gómez-Peña y Roberto Sifuentes

Se cruzan canyons   en el templo de confessions.
Language lies   across the barbed lines,
piles of its bodies   pierced y pinchados.
No one evades   the essentialist evangels,
the Other who offers   his objectified body
to the river rats   who ride his wetback,
the coro de coyotes   who crave his flesh,
the wheyfaced who whisper   their sin in his ear,
the translators who trap   and trade his tongue,
la raza who receive him,   la raza who repel him.

In this chamber the chill   of chicken flesh—
pollito mojado   picoso y picado,
the black body   bag of the repatriated.
Here the distorted words   of debutants y do-gooders,
of know-no-betters   y neo-nazis,
of Beowulfs and other   born-again beasts,
of sandaled sombreros   sleeping under cacti,
of Machiavelian   mentes y mouths
of anthropological   autoethnography,
of pretend pachucas   peeling their layers,
of preachers and poets   with puckered lips
of the misused multi-   cultural machinery,
of the Hispanic hodgepodge   hiding their Indio,
of the Quetzalcoatls   concealing their conqueror
de la migra meando   marking its turf.

Here, the hemistiched   hemispheres blend,
a vacuum of voices   absorbed in the velvet
paintings of slick   y sexy santos,
of the Aztec icon   at the altar of Aztlán
tripping and turning   transvestite warrior,
of the cyber-Cholo   stripping down—Simón!
The Vato loco's liquid   eye lures us
over borders, their blurred   tumbling barriers

calling us to come   stare into the cage—
jaula de joda   aquí juntándonos—
the table turned   and tacked to the wall,
lit with votives   licking our luscious
breakfast bowl   of cucarachas on their backs
squirming to free   their feet and fly.

Through Arms and Hands

I.
Young hands manipulate
brushes like marionettes
        in a whirl. They bend
                the retina's mirror
        into the world beat
of a street mural:

Revolution lifts a sister's fist,
a brother's clanking wrists
        beneath a red moon—
cracked disk spinning into shadow,
the static of her profile
        ripping an unpredictable skip
through the fleshy folds of sky.

Revolution squints at light falling
        between floorboards.
Under their creaking,
        she hides peaking
at the treaded soles who would sink
        tracks above the bridge
of her brow, crush the bones
        beneath her eyes, fine
as the fiberglass in a fish back.

Revolution turns back

to the hills, dragging his limp leg
        through the dust like a satchel
        of citrus plucked
from land that sprouts
barbed trees between its wire knees,
        and shakes pellets from its shoes.

Revolution's got the soul for blues,
a jazz jones, raggae rhythm,
syllabic hip hop, bebop,
a mambo, samba, bomba y rhumba,
cumbia con clave de salsa,
        scat a phat rap back, tap tickety-tack,
        wail back a throaty Delta Blues
        that rode the rails to the relief
        mosaic of Chicago skyline,
guitar strings picking the glint
        of bottle caps and green glass,
        shards of brass blowing
up fire escapes
                down tenement reverberation
rippling off the rim of the hoop,
        your life chalked into tar,
summer steam bubbling up.

        Rebellion tags in cryptic glyph,
        riffs, but never bites
        another's arc of mist.

II.
Revolution is no man's flag.

III.
A screech unfurls
        from raven's open beak
        pointed like rage
                into the split sky.

The raven-haired women sew
bullets into blouses,
     grind smoke into stone,
        sing the comal's hiss
        as they roll us out on the metate
like a sheet of masa.

Prayer curls around the red nest
     in our chests
like a rattler warming eggs,
        then stretches, unspined,
       a camouflaged line slashing
           into the green-gold blades.

Revolution is a blade
cleaned by the tongue of God.

Marta Collazo (Pluma)

These poems are dedicated to my sister Dora,
who died tragically and who taught me how to live.

What Is Good Magic/Good Voodoo

When she cooks
pigeon peas and yellow
rice
the kitchen smells like
congas
red onions
chiles
moje
monfongo.

When she cooks pigeon peas
and yellow rice
the congas smell like
sweet plátanos
cumin seed
bay leaves
cilantro
achiote.

When she cooks
pigeon peas and yellow rice
the kitchen
sounds like sofrito
good people
sipping
coconut rum.

Nudity
Is raw
Lacks imagination
That peculiar
Exercise
Where contorted
Bodies
Move in anticipation
Of some form of
Relief.
Talk to me
Talk dirty
Good sex
Is a slow flame
That touches nothing
Unless told to do so
A wo
Needs to be wooed
Like an entrée
Licked from bottom
To top
Then she won't mind
If u spank her soft
With a hair brush
Sex is somehow
More
Like a home cooked
Meal
A wo wants to be wooed
By time
And soul
Great sex
Takes turns because
Fantasy
Is much
Greater than the act
Of penetration
A wo
Wants to be wooed

In a sumo house
Where a large man
Runs a bath
Reads poetry
Rolls grapefruit
From the other side
Of the room
Lays her clothes out
Dresses
One garter
At a time
Waits
For proof
Of satisfaction
All over her face
Between her legs
A good sumo
Will peel layers
In search of truth
And pleasure
To get
We must all learn to give
To give we must
All learn to receive
One finger at a time
One eyelid at a time
One eyebrow at a time
One hair at a time
Talk to me
Talk dirty
Great
Sex is a slow flame
That touches
Nothing unless told
To do so.

Because blood is thinner
than mud
and flows more easily;
because Juan Luis Guerra,
Frederico García Lorca,
Rubén Blades
could all wear fedoras,
linen,
even a gardenia
(although none like you);
because only the elegant
could smoke a cigarette,
seduce you
to forget cancer;
because brown is
maple cappuccino,
Cuervo Gold
and so are you;
because palm trees
and guayaberas
stand straight
the way caballeros
are supposed to;
because of hot spinning fans,
black and white movies,
staircases,
gabardine trousers,
Fred Astaire
sliding on art deco tiles
smiling that sugar cane smile;
because we all have to build
our own Mafia,
the world gave me
a brother for a gift—
because blood
is thinner than mud
and flows more easily.

Daisy Cubias

Guerra

Oigo
    El cansancio de la muerte
        Tocando
            Las puertas y ventanas
                Traicionado
El día inaccesible
        Terminó de repente
            Multiplicando
Hombres militares
        Los brutales
            Amantes de la muerte.

                    ℰ ℰ ℰ

War

I hear
    The weariness of death
        Knocking
            at doors and windows
                Betrayed
The inaccessible day
        Abruptly ended
            Multiplying
Military men
        The brazen
            Lovers of death.

Political Exiles

Maíz seeds in asphalt,
corn fields grow in black cement
weaving yesterday's thoughts.

Voices whisper memories
in silence,
lives broken by cold
dead winters.
Innocent souls betrayed
under a heavy rain of papers,
laws give false hope
to children who eat
the left over shadows
of stale bread.

Exported assassins
hired to wait in dark alleys
help death steal lives.
Frustrated exiles
hold back their sorrow
listening to memories
of eternal gunfire.

Some are strangled very slowly,
pain waiting to ambush
their hearts,
love buried in clouds
of court indecisions.
Dictators
act like gentlemen
when they visit foreign countries.

Churches divided
by walls of indifference
and silence,
religions pull strings of gold
in the name of God

while political exiles wait
for the next
presidential election.

Past

I go back to the time
when I was a young girl
and grandfather was
alive,
telling me about
Tlaloc and Quetzalcoatl—
the gods who protected
the Indians, the Pipiles,
the corn fields,
and the villages—
stories about campesinos,
Ciguanabas,*
Cipitios y Justo Juez de la Noche—*
the folklore of my country
that will always
live in me.

*Ciguanabas, Cipitios and Justo Juez de la Noche are part of Salvadoran
Folklore history.

Silvia Divinetz

Auf Zweifel / To Doubt

"Eine Stirn, so hart wie ein Pflasterstein, und schlägt los auf Zweifel" /
"A brain as hard as a cobblestone, hurled at doubt"
—E. Canetti translated by John Hargraves

To dream was not enough
to witness was not enough
to denounce was not enough
to spit at their faces was not enough
to shake our fists was not enough
to parade our placards was not enough
to face their horses was not enough
to burn our books at that hour
    between the fall of day
    and the knock on the door was not enough.

Turned to cobblestones,
polarized, sharpened, vectorial,
no white light but a single wave,
brains were hurled at doubt
so that all doubt be shattered.

As for those
who could not choose
those
whose brains refused
    to be weapons,
who were afraid,
caught between
    the left arm of outrage
    and the right arm of wisdom,
those whose ancestors' bones
    littered the common graves,
and then
those who saw their children hurl
    their hardened brains

only to see them whirl
like boomerangs back into their hands,
and those who never saw their children hurl,
and those who never saw their children again,

we have taken doubt in our arms
and with a ragged cloth
                ceaselessly wash its face.

Call

They say bones call.
Like clouds' shadows, they call,
like bees spurred from broken lives
or a child's open mouth.
They say like thunder under the edge of a storm, they call
all night long, or like the white star-shaped flowers
matting the space under dense oak leaves,
even when one would barely fill
the moon under my small fingernail.

They say in the Northern lakes, they call, in cities—
in Toronto,
in Chicago by the river mounds,
in Los Angeles white under its soil
dark as bodies,
in the verticle jungles of New York luscious
over those exiled, kidnapped,
escaped from famines
to the metal breath of the factories,
in the garbage dumps
on the outskirts of Buenos Aires
and deep under the muddy waters
of the Río de la Plata,
from the sky like birds in soundless flight
·suddenly

without feathers
or the wave of a hand,
without a gaze
spiraling down as they fall.

They say that if you programmed satellites
to seek them out from high above
as they did to map dry ancient riverbeds
underneath the Earth's surface,
ice under the moon's,
you could not see bones:
only a solid whiteness
all the way to the core.

Iguazú

And they fall
from great heights
into the dark vocal stones

like the memory of a loved one's voice
deep in the humid fauces of Iguazú
clouds and mist
        stung
by the infinite crine
falling into the lap of the boscage.

What pheromones float in the air?
What ancient call,
        desire
to bare the body thirsty
arms entwined with the green
fingers of the foliage?
Oh to fall unfastened
pores open,
into the copulating scents
of the rain forest.

Aullando

En la lengua de Cervantes
        sus voces aún conmigo:

        de Azorín
        de Juana
        de Gabriela
        —Pablo
        —Federico

la voz de mi madre
y de Alfonsina,*
"que está la tarde ya sobre mi vida
y esta pasión tan ciega y desmedida
la he perdido, Señor, haciendo versos."

Qué absurdo destino de cuyanas,
yo aullando sola en la brumosa luz
lacustre de las mañanas de Minneapolis
        mientras ella—abierto su costado—
                caminó sola
                bajo las saladas
                olas voraces
                de las estrellas atlánticas.

❧ ❧ ❧

* *Alfonsina Storni—poeta de San Juan, Argentina, que murió ahogada.*

Howling

In the tongue of Cervantes
                    their voices are still with me:

        de Azorín
        de Juana
        de Gabriela
        —Pablo
        —Federico

my mother's voice
and Alfonsina's, *
"dusk already falling on my life
and this passion so stubborn and so blind,
I have spent, my Lord, composing verses."

What an absurd midwesterner's fate:
I howling alone in the dim,
lacunar light of Minneapolis mornings
                    while she—side open wound—
                              walked alone
                              under the salty
                              voracious waves
                              of Atlantic stars.

Alfonsina Storni—poet from San Juan, Argentina, who drowned.

Oigo el pasar de la vida

"The days pass, and sometimes
I hear the passing of life."
—*R.M. Rilke*

a veces
como gotas de lluvia
como respiraciones
como el sol recorriendo
        mi ventana
barriendo los trazos
del día

con sus manos delgadas
ya nudosas
en lana blanca y roja
mi madre
tejió una manta para mis hijas
mientras contemplaba
como gotas de lluvia
como respiraciones
la vida pasando

los ojos perdidos
en la distancia
como oye un jazmín
un arándano
una brizna
el susurro de las hojas
el abedul que plantamos
en el último viaje de mi hermano
apretado entre las verjas
        de las casas
el susurro
barriendo la memoria
trazos abandonados
del día

como gotas de lluvia

a veces
trabajosas respiraciones
mi madre en un lecho
mirando las rojas baldosas
la escalera descubierta
en el patio
enmarcando
un trozo triangular de cielo
la súbita marea inundando
sus pulmones fatigados
agua y sal
cada alveolo
rodeado

como un grano de arena
o tal vez
contemplando la bóveda
de plátanos añosos
sobre el balcón de mi pieza
la calle atestada
los autos volviendo del trabajo
en el temprano anochecer de Agosto
los rugidos apagándose
yéndose
barriendo trazos
oyendo
como pasaba la vida
los trazos
abandonados del día
como gotas de lluvia
como respiraciones
cesando

I Hear the Passing of Life

"The days pass, and sometimes
I hear the passing of life."
                    —R.M. Rilke

at times
like raindrops
like breath
like the sun moving
          through my window
sweeping traces
from the day

with her knuckled
thin hands
in red and white wool
my mother knitted a blanket
for my daughters
contemplating
like raindrops
like breath
the passing of life

eyes unfocused
on the distance
the way a jasmine hears
a bilberry
a leaf of grass
the rustle of the leaves
the river birch we planted
on my brother's last trip
crushed between the fences
          of the houses
the whisper
sweeping the memory
abandoned traces
from the day

like raindrops

at times
with labored breathing
my mother on a bed
watching the red tiles
the open stair
in the patio
framing
a triangular slice of sky
the sudden tide flooding
her jaded lungs
salt and water
every alveolus
surrounded
like a grain of sand

or perhaps
contemplating the vault
of ancient sycamores
over my room's balcony
the crowded street
cars returning from work
the early dusk of August
the dull roar
leaving
sweeping traces
hearing
the passing of life
abandoned
traces of the day
like raindrops
like breath
ceasing

Venessa Maria Fuentes

Cebollas

Mi abuelita dice que cuando
la cebolla
te hace llorar, es porque es
macho. Cebolla hombre.
The men bring
tears to the eyes, she says. And, from
what I understand,
from the way certain wrinkles
lie on her face when she is sad and
full of her Bolivia
I do not doubt this.
But we are different women.
Onions to me are not the same thing.
Our shared names
do not fit the
same way in our mouths. No importa—we still know what
the other means.
I wonder:
how many onions
has my abuela chopped in her life? How many
paper shells peeled away to make the
fingers and palms so smooth.
She has no more fingerprints. They've worked
themselves inside out and now
face her blood rather than the blade.
She is my mother tongue, where I come from.
I breathe deeply enough to
touch the bottoms of my lungs
when I know she's been cooking.
Check her eyes to see if she's been crying,
tear stain on a napkin.
Abuela's history
adds another shell to mine.
I am looking forward to the day when
my wrinkly hands can be so calm.

Hermanita, Hermanota

She
would have been a good
little sister.
I think of her all skinny fingered
and rootless like me.
I like to think she is thinking
of me somewhere.
Hermanita, hermanota.
I am romancing the idea,
wanting more than a global sisterhood kinda thing.
I'm talking about genetics.
Biology. A shared curve here or there
to the fingerprints.
A secret language and
giggles underneath the sheets.
Would we have similar memories of our
mother's belly sleeping
in the backs of our heads?
She would have been my
tiny anchor. I, her mixed up ocean.
We, searching for home. Finding it in the
movements pigeons follow as they fly,
by the church,
in a circle.
Our skinny fingers
prying open the dried lips
of our history. Demanding re-entry.
Kissing warmth and blood back in.

I believe she is out there.
Hermanita, escúchame.
There are too many colors
wrapped around each other.
Too much mutt blood. So much that it
mixes even with the earth,
con esta tierra callada, like water.
It moves with ferocity

underneath the surface. It moves
because it has to.
To find home
kneel down.
Put your tiny ear to the ground.
Put your finger on your pulse.
These will match, the currents of our mutt
blood moving.
Qué bonito.
I will meet you there
at our home sin fronteras.
Will recognize you by the dirt on your knees.

Birthday

for Sandi

I.
I want a diamond for the hollow of my neck.
Just a small one, a newborn
birthmark. Give me vases of
flowers, the kind a kindergartner would
scribble using fat crayons.
Red, yellow, orange petals.
Some with freckles. Your shoulders falling
over me. A nest of dragon's heads knocking together, long necks
of cool green drinking up water like mad.

II.
Could we paint the bedroom blue?

Listen, we could hide sapphires in the boxspring.
Thread peacock feathers on fish line—hang them
to look like angels. Like rain. In one corner,
a tank with turtle inside, happy with her
warm puddle, her bowl of cold fruit and leaves.
Callas singing.
And you perfect.
And me wishing.

III.
My friend, we will go to the opera. Bring the baby.
It's my birthday.
Wear your velvet dress, I'll string a crown of lights
for each of us. On a Sunday in September the
lights go down and the story begins.
You and I singing along
just as we had joked.
Making up words and the child sitting between us
combing her hair.

Pinki

para Tatiana

Give me your pinki,
mujer.
I promise you five snowflakes
each perfect,
six-sided
bien pretty kept in a box.
I'm telling you,
the moment sparrows,
all bone and bread,
start their noise in the trees
        that frida-blue hour the best time for prayer
I know the North Shore
in you—
lake water, two rocks,
an afghan caught between cushions.
I know Colombia
in you,
that pearl on your finger from
so far away,
mother tongue wrapped tight in memory,
bit of white gold,
one dozen daffodils.

Rina García

Blue Sky

These afternoons with my red polished fingernails,
I scratch the blue, blue sky.
Revealing once bandaged dreams,
licking festering wounds,
I grab a pedestrian cloud
to soothe and sop up
what life tends to spill over.
I exfoliate daily

from my spirit-hurting cells,
some of them have names like yours,
like hers and his.
But always, after doing this,
I scratch that blue, blue sky.

Sometimes, just sometimes,
in a rhythmically hip motion
I dance deliverance
under the wounded sky.
Laughing,
knowing that I've reached
up, up, up,
leaving reminders that I was there.

Nursery Rhyme

Daddy do,
Daddy do,
Do wear your gray hat,
gray suit.
Pour the beer in a tall clear glass
read el periódico.

Daddy me,
Daddy me,
Will you take me?
Pressed, folded and sectioned,
a nine-year-old handkerchief
in your suit coat pocket.

Daddy laugh,
Daddy laugh,
Shoes hidden in the oven,
playful past.
If you find them
you can leave.

You left.
One woman,
Two children,
No regrets.
Until twenty-five years later...

You returned.
When your knees can't bend
and your body is crippled
by the offense.

The cycle of "vas a ver,"
justice is complete.
Daddy's niña,
Daddy's niña
says you're dead.

Jagged Days

Living on the edge of a rusty razor blade, slipping off, soon.
Teetering on one foot, then another,
stainless steel tightrope cuts into my petite foot.
Is tomorrow the day that I'll fall on a cloud
of dead prayers?
All said in vain,
all done in vain.
I'm all done swallowing
another Darvon.
This nagging pain that stretches
across my abdomen has tentacles that seize my
heart and split it open like a nutcracker.

Squish!
I'm convinced that tomorrow,
or sometime next week,
my soon to be ex-husband and his friend
will nudge me over the blade.
Tonight, I'll lick some of the rust and
get accustomed to the taste.
Tomorrow, my words will have two meanings,
being blamed for this or that,
accusations of unfaithfulness.

I confess.
I profess, I'm living on the edge of a rusty razor blade,
falling onto my bed with no shame.

Juana Iris Goergen

Homenaje a Silvio #2

A punta de malabarismos
sobrevive
Abrazada a si misma
ineludible
Amarrada a sus plantas
en su propio lugar
el único
el preciso
El canto de los grillos
y su canto es el mismo:
Había una vez una mujer dormida
que echó su cuerpo al vuelo
y no hubo red
ni público
ni cuerdas
En plena transparencia
y sin tapujos
su húmeda blancura
su dureza rosada
su centro de equilibrio
abierto a todos los peligros
como el de despertar cada mañana
lluvia a prueba de agua
fuego a prueba de llama
Perdida en diccionarios
masticando palabras
como si fueran uvas
almendras
pan caliente o carne cruda
oscura y descreída
aprendió a ser feliz con las palabras
creyendo a pierna abierta
en el amor a manos llenas
para ver

si siendo a carne viva
puede salir con vida
de esta vida.

လာ လာ လာ

Homage to Silvio #2

Juggling on the verge
she survives
Embracing herself
inescapable
Tied to her plants
in her own place
the only one
the precise one
The song of the crickets
and her song are the same:
Once there was a woman asleep
who threw her body to flight
and there was no net
no public
no rope
In pure transparency
and without secrecy
her humid whiteness
her pink hardness
her center of equilibrium
open to all dangers
like that of awakening each morning
rain proofed against water
fire proofed against flame
Lost in dictionaries
chewing words
as if they were grapes
almonds
warm bread or raw meat
dark and disbelieving
she learned to be happy with the words

believing open legged
in love, her hands full
to see
if being in raw flesh
she can exit alive
this life.

La Maga

Era el viaje
de mi lugar
en un avión de papel
Era mirarte
como un pez fuera del agua
como el fuego
al hombre primitivo
diciendo:
"en el cielo, hay un infierno para los tristes"
Era extrañar
a la mujer temprana
de había una vez
Era volver
a tus ojos de maga
con diarios y cuentos de Cortázar
deciendo:
"el amarillo es el último color"
Y era mirarte
voraz
como un monje antiguo
frente a un libro incunable
pero no era la muerte.
La muerte
es la toalla
que acaricia la desnudez
como una lengua cansada
o las letras rojas en la portada del Vogue
o sólo su color

o el espacio entre cada una
o la *o* con su rostro vacío.

෴ ෴ ෴

The Maga

It was the journey
from my place to yours
in a paper airplane
It was to look at you
like a fish out of water
like fire
at primordial man
saying:
"In heaven, there is a hell for the miserable"
It was to miss
the early woman
of once upon a time
It was to return
to your Maga eyes
with diaries and stories of Cortázar
saying:
"Yellow is the final color"
And it was to look at you
famished
like an ancient monk
before an incurable book
but it was not death.
Death
is the towel
that caresses this nudity
like a tired tongue
or the red letters on the cover of Vogue
or only their color
or the space between each one
or the *o* with its empty face.

Reconquista

Cuando los trenes
suben por mi garganta
ahogando un grito,
no hay máquina ni método
el ruido inventa el tiempo
y cuanto escribo
a grito enmudecido
en otra lengua me desnombro
       "Oak Park" "Lincoln Park"
         "Logan Square"
       "Green Line" "Brown Line"
       "Tous Les Matins Du Monde"
grita alguien furera de contexto
y yo
de tanto no estar
en dos lugares
pierdo el centro.

Desnombrada
ni siquiera Walt Whitman
osaría intentar reconocerme
mi nombre es un manojo de huesos
llanto de mastiles
sobre las arillas
nada contiene esta figura de mujer
colonizada
una ternura incierta
un reloj ensombrecido
un animal que piensa
un ojo que se asoma
al balcón de otros ojos
que vive de miradas
de otras miradas
y que se vuelve a ti Walt Whitman
y que vuelve a llamarte
de vacío a vacío.

Desnombrados
dime, dime, Walt Whitman
¿qué edad tendrán estas orillas
que se roban mi cuerpo poco a poco?
y estas manos
que no se asombran
y estos ojos
que se desploman a mis pies
¿qué edad tendrán?
dime, dímelo tú
Walt Whitman
que entre ruido de trenes
me preguntas
¿quién soñó a esta mujer
que pule y afila
los hilos de su escoba?
a esta mujer
que es agua en movimiento
alrededor de una isla
imaginaria
que entró por las paredes
grabando su escritura
en las ventanas
y preguntándose
¿quién te soñó a ti
Walt Whitman?
entrando solo al templo
de un reinito transparente
que me quitó mi país
mi país
mi país
que me quitó mi país
que también se pregunta
¿quién soñó a esta mujer
que va cambiando los muros y las puertas
y que camina un sueño
que resienten los ancestros y el "status"?

Pobres

pobres tú y yo
Walt Whitman este reloj no tiene péndulo que asista
déjame darle
Participación a la crisis
que la mañana es nueva
y un animal desnudo me vincula
a los ojos de una niña diminuta
y tú
que me andas lejos
debajo de la voz
y yo
a oscuras
yo
a gritos
comida a tiendas
por el ojo hirviente que me canta
no existo
y al desnombrarme
y al renombrarte a ti
Walt Whitman
desaparezco intacta
y me destierro
me destierro a un poema.

෴ ෴ ෴

Reconquest
Translated by Silvia Tandeciarz

When the trains
rise up my throat
drowning a scream,
there is no machine, no method
noise invents time
and what I write
in muted cry
in another tongue I unname myself
        "Oak Park" "Lincoln Park"
          "Logan Square"
        "Green Line" "Brown Line"
        "Tous Les Matins Du Monde"
screams someone out of context
and I
from so much not being
in two places
lose my center.

Unnamed
not even Walt Whitman
would dare try to recognize me
my name is a heap of bones
the weeping of masts
upon all shores
nothing contains this figure of a woman
colonized
an uncertain tenderness
a clock in shadow
an animal that thinks
an eye that glances
at the balcony of other eyes
that feeds off looks
off other looks
and turns back to you
Walt Whitman
and calls you once again

from emptiness to emptiness.

Unnamed
tell me, tell me Walt Whitman
how old are these shores
that steal my body little by little?
and these hands
that are not awed
and these eyes
that topple to my feet
how old can they be?
tell me, tell me yourself
Walt Whitman
who between the noise of trains
asks me
who dreamt this woman
polishing and sharpening
the threads of her broom?
this woman
that is water in motion
around the imaginary
island
who entered through the walls
recording her writing
on the windows
and asking herself
who dreamt you
Walt Whitman?
entering alone into the temple
of a transparent kingdom
that took away my country
my country
my country
that took away my country
that also asks itself
who dreamt this woman
who goes about changing the walls and the doors
and walks a dream
that the ancestors and the political status resent?

Poor us
poor you and I
Walt Whitman
this clock has no pendulum to help
let me enjoy
this crisis
now that the morning is new
and a naked animal ties me
to the eyes of a diminuitive girl
and you
who wanders in me from far away
beneath the voice
and I
in the dark
I
screaming
devoured geography
by the seething eye that sings me
I do not exist
and in unnaming me
and in renaming you
Walt Whitman
I disappear intact
and exile myself
exile my self to a poem.

Lisa Guedea Carreño

Villanelle for La Llorona

Dark earth haunts her young by night,
Over cribs and cradles creeps
And crouches in shadows of gray-dimmed sight.

She bathes pale moon in thick blue-white;
Through wool blankets moon's beams seep.
Dark earth haunts her young by night.

Curtains blown in flutter-flight
Beckon child in hushed half-sleep
And crouch in shadows of gray-dimmed sight.

Closets and corners of cubbyhole delight
Turn into caverns, dim and deep.
Dark earth haunts her young by night.

Creaks and scratches hiss and bite,
Tree-limbed creatures lurch and leap
And crouch in shadows of gray-dimmed sight.

And children wake in fevered fright,
While mothers pray their souls to keep,
For dark earth haunts her young by night
And crouches in shadows of gray-dimmed sight.

These Days

These days she lives
largely on small doses
of medication and maintenance:
Fill up with gas
on the way to work late.
Eat another vegetable today.
Leave early for
the shrink, and on the way
pick up the dry cleaning,
cheap wine from the corner store,
yesterday's paper to scan.
Tears and sex late in the day
and a cigarette in bed
will help her sleep tonight.

Sometimes in the
early half-light of dark,
she fills the house with sound—bass vibrates,
drum downbeats the
angry-woman questions
with no right answers. She knows, feels it
spill from speakers
rushing through halls, down stairs,
into spare rooms and closets he cleared out,
seeping into every crack
and dusty empty corner
that once held his essence.

But this liquid gray
rage is a balm too.
She spreads it like
a salve, feels skin absorb it
burning first, then numbing the surface
just deep enough
to last until morning.

Prioritizing pain is an art

and a saving grace
these days.

Pennies

Pennies, my curly-red-brown-haired love brings
Little moons of burnt gold, rusted sun tops;
In the milk glass mug on my window ledge they drop,
As playful penny metal clinking rings.
Each evening he passes, into my open window he peeks,
With a hand full of the day's collected gifts for me.
He laughs and teases, begs a kiss—his fee
For brown-gold buttons, these dimples from his cheeks.

Oh, wispy-whiskered boy, why give pennies
To me? Am I your mother, that I must care
For these moons of your soft-cheeked nights of youth again?
They are no more than copper curls of your hair.
I can no longer laugh at childhood's penny joys,
Nor give my love for the copper moons of boys.

Roadkill

On the edge
of the road
where the shoulder crumbles
stuck to gravel
and asphalt chunks
clinging to what won't scatter,
I look away
and hold my breath
while passing to the right side.

But particles linger,
float in the air above,
wait for warmth, open pores
to reabsorb what's left.

What is the
half life of
a life no longer lived?
Habits and ghosts:
are they banished
images come back to haunt,
or are they scraps
salvaged from the
rituals of rage?

If you want all of me
you get the faint spirits
that hover in the air
around me, wanting you
to inhale.

Cristina Herrera

Children of the Ancients

for Keewaydinoquay Peschel
—in memoriam—

we are children of the ancients
what flows through our veins
is memory

trust what you know
listen to all you remember
the past walks beside us
we must move forward together

we are the children of the ancients
memory is an intricate web
invisible threads connect us
one to another

the waters flow over the face
of this place
and they are inhabited
the trees translate and join
with branches above and below
the stones are living records
taking everything down

we are children of the ancients
approaching our rite of passage
dreaming of what might be

capacities lie dormant in our DNA
we don't understand 90 percent
of our flowering brains
and label the clues
metaphysics

do caterpillars grasp the significance
when they hear the beat of a wing
and see a splash of color fly by

we are children of the ancients
truth falls like rain all around us
feel water caress on its way to the ground

Seven Words

the listening
passes through
everyone

are you
everyone

passes through you
are the listening

you are
everyone
listening
through the passes

listening
everyone you are
passes through

the listening

passes
through everyone

are you
the listening

everyone
passes through
passes
through everyone

the listening
you are

listening
through everyone

the passes
are you
listening

you are
listening
through
the passes

everyone
the listening
passes through
you

are listening

are you listening

Wisdom Is Language*

Looking out across the water
waves weave wonder in the night
we had poems and songs then
they put us on alert
our explanations are insufficient
there may be more going on than we thought

I.

On a day like today
the wind that blew
the rocks that knew
breathe together
conspire
in my mind
a word
takes shape

it is movement
breath
heart
vibration

it is occult
hidden
covered
is it time to recover
we found a way to live without memory
it is time to remember

On a day like today
the wind that blew
the stones that knew
breathe together
conspire
in my mind

a word
takes shape

II.

an image caught
within a word
turns in our mind

unseen hands
like wings
stir the dust
of settled thought
into dancing streams
of dappled light

a walk in time
we mark this place
with fluid scent
of memory dreaming
in footprints
and rotting wood
moist earthen floor
where we once stood
beneath a tree
Mpingo singing
whispered melodies
branches mapping
the hushed seasons

III.

rocks powder beneath our feet
stones turn to sand
our open hand
releases dreams
like seeds of dandelion

milkweed to Milky Way
their power
blooms in stars
which pierce the night

we cry the tears of vision
meeting sea
waves of memory
rise in tides of
thunderous history
eroding molten thought
turned cold and hard
to start
again
a spinning world
a spoken word
suspended in
the ocean space
waiting to be heard

IV.

I long for the day
when the words I say
carved from the Earth
illumined by star's light
are enough

when the movement
of one breath
can change
weather patterns
and minds

I long for the day
when the oceans
flow through our veins
and the languages we speak

all come from one word

I long for the day
when our feet know
where they're going
our hands become
the body of thanksgiving

when the beauty
of our time here
is the only dance we know
and we sing
ideas into existence

the eyes create distance
the heart knows better

the choice is to remember
the forgetting has been done

The phrase "Wisdom is language" is attributed to María Sabina.

Ixtaccíhuatl

Origins

I.
Everything she lives is propelled
by the momentum of memory and México.

In the yellow house it began;
on an iron bed draped in bleached muslin,
Ana María in attendance, braided black hair
at the nape of her neck, sure brown hands ribbed with veins.

Backdrop: a small square room,
sky-blue flaking paint filled with the scent
of rubbing alcohol, sunlight filtered
through uneven blinds.

Small young woman on the bed,
face flushed with effort, dark hair
spread on the pillow. Quiet moans
escaped her lips, afterthoughts to pain.

II.
Dark blue-faced girl arrived,
self-made noose at neck
cord tight—unable or unwilling
to cry or breathe, eyes shut tight,
small fists battling air.

She preferred the floating cocoon;
distant sounds murmuring, music
all things muted, toned down.

III.
Years later, that same child

becomes a woman who only senses absence.
Unfilled spaces call her attention on paper
as do pauses between spoken words.

On her dresser, in a leather frame
the face of a frightened child peers out
captured in black and white,
encased in plastic, a murky green,
color of the Río Bravo at twilight.

Soy Bella

I am beautiful because I am a poem
made up of lines begun by my ancestors,
who danced in flickering firelight
to the sounds of hand-carved flutes
and prayer rattles, conch shells, singing drums.

Feather garbed forefathers bled ruby fountains onto earth and stone
died flowery deaths that I might rise from their ashes—complete
what they had begun before being slain by invaders;
demented & diseased dogs, rabid with hunger for sparkling rocks
melted into yellow liquid, virulent as blood in their veins
that contaminated and killed everything they touched.

I am beautiful because I am Adelita, daughter of revolution,
bullets strapped across my chest, cooking over campfires,
scent of gunpowder permeating air, mingling with the odors
of sweat, the sound of firing canons—
beautiful because when I died, I died like the men, standing.

Granted Moments

These are granted moments
son momentos regalados
don't search for reasons.

Aroma of cinnamon coffee
breaths that rise and fall
your own, the faint scent
of someone you love.

Your hands clasp a mug
like the upturned face
of a weeping child;
you kiss the rim.

Water envelopes skin
and you recall raindrops
on damp earth in México
dulces y raspas
la feria de San Juan—

Veins in your hands
are roads you've traveled;
changes in your face
watermarks of time, ceases
ghosts of laughter.

Por la ventana entra luz
y esa luz trae paz.

Sunlight on your face
warms you, recalls the kiss
of a past lover.

The baby you've held
becomes you sleeping
en los brazos de tu madre
and all you know
her embrace.

Lorena Rosalia Manzo

Empanadas

The hacienda.
The smell of soap.
Ten women are running around the kitchen.
It's six in the morning;
they just finished showering
sending their children to school
and, with a few wet hairs
sticking to the back of their necks,
they are already arranging pots and pans
para el almuerzo.

Ten women,
all barefoot.
The smell of bananas and coconuts
impregnates their souls.

Ten women,
all barefoot.
the sound of their knives
cutting tomatoes and remolachas
so sharply
almost with a vengeance.

Ten women,
all barefoot,
there are pineapples here and there,
pineapples, the baby sisters of palm trees
under which they were once desired.

Ten women,
all barefoot,
the bittersweet freshness of limes
reminds the ten barefoot women
of the kisses of ten men

who told them once under the palm trees
that they would never end up barefoot
running around in a kitchen at six in the morning.

I ask my mother what they are doing,
why the ten barefoot women don't
go outside and enjoy the day at the beach.
She said they are too busy washing vegetables,
preparing soup and the meat,
baking flan for dessert
and making empanadas.

"A woman must cook for her husband
to keep him by her side."
I look at the ten barefoot women and think,
"Fuck your empanadas,
when I grow up I'll order pizza."

Sure I'll Answer Your Questions

Yes, I like to wear black.
No, I am not goth.
Yes, I read the tarot cards,
I'll read your tobacco too.
No, I am not a witch.
Yes, I drink.
No, I am not an alcoholic.
Yes, I wear make-up,
I feel very feminine.
No, I am not submissive.
Yes, I wear tight clothes.
No, I am not a hooker.

Yes, I speak Spanish.
No, I am not Mexican.
Yes, I like enchiladas and tequila,

but really, I am not Mexican.
I am South American.
No, I didn't live in the Amazon jungle.
Yes, we do have T.V.
No, we don't eat human meat.

This is my family,
Yes, we are Latin.
Yes, we throw big parties.
Yes, some Latinos drive nice cars.
No, we are not all drug dealers.

No, I am not married.
No, really it's O.K.
I am not depressed about it,
trust me.

Yes, I've had boyfriends,
we broke up.
No, I am not depressed about that either.
No, I don't need a man.
No, I am not a lesbian.
I like men,
I just don't need one.

Yes, I am a woman.
Yes, I am alone.
No, you don't intimidate me.

Sin

Ave María Purísima,
Sin pecado concebida.

Forgive me father
for I have sinned.

Against my husband's wishes
I have been actually thinking,
thinking if my life could be any different.

I have been exposing my pink toenails
to the men at the market
when I go there early in the morning
to buy eggs and fresh tomatoes.

I opened the forbidden book last night
the one that made me question.
I touched forbidden skin last night
the one that makes me desire.

His hair is long and black,
like the time I have waited;
his skin is cinnamon and grass
his arms pillows of passion.

Last night I let my white breasts
touch the childless moon
while he let me ride on the young
forest of his affections.

Forgive me father
for I have sinned
I am a woman
and I have been thinking.

Silence

I am expecting nothing tonight,
only Silence;
Silence may keep me company.

The sudden sound of the heater activating scared me
like the sound of an earthquake
while Silence and I were abandoned at the Andes.

It was midnight,
it was silent
just like tonight.

We want to be able to hear the
breeze traveling through
our eyelashes.

We want to have a mute conversation
with that man digging into the garbage can.

We want to feel certain
that good and evil can still
rest safely beneath our skirts.

Then,
we want to be left alone;
Silence and I.

A woman needs her space.

The phone rings.

Janessa María-Diego

She Got Bird

She got crow bottom.
She got rooster on top.
She got droopy turkey pressed against her middle.
She got crane twining between her legs.

She got owl hypnotizing her nipples.
She got hummingbird messing her hair.
She got dove vibrating against her throat.

She got tiny men in bird masks
Dangling from her fingertips.
She got feather tongue.

She got red hawk biting her lower lip.
She got shivers for the hawk.

Dear Manita

left you
for that
slut
I hear
there are snakes
who bite
and later
you beg
to remember what
venom made you
forget—What?
your conejita
not blonde enough
nipples too black
and that line
on your belly—
Who put that
there? Wait
'til he tries
living without
your words
licking his
neck pillowy
verses against
his face
he will reach
for your dark
eyebrows like lost
rhymes beg you
to put your long
poem under his pants
I say do it
little sister
but piss on it
first

To a Spaniard (I Explain the Midwest)

here I dwell in a low place
in a mist thick with willows
mysterious intimates
you will never see
voices
your voices
settle in every corner
provocative
chill

I tell you here
the creeks have flooded
surfacing small things
mysterious intimates
you will never see
winter's dry reeds drift into the fish roe
abandoned shell of caddis fly
empty
exquisite
rolls in the current
here, tiny turbulence

here I live immersed
in the small
inundated
solvent
eye-level with
the edge of the world
even this snail
upended
suspended on the surface
of the stream
does not have
my view

When it comes let me be ready to receive

when it comes
and I am leaning full weight
against the door
when it comes
one hand knocking
fist
shoulder against hinge
let me give
in
it will come
force of wings cutting air
cries falling on my face like hail
let it smother me
wing of hawk
claws on thighs
above
my voice dove in the rain
when I take it full force
stinging on my cheeks
melting on my neck
when I taste it
salt and snow
let me be
extendida
arms spread
wings against snow
ready
ready
boca abierta
to receive

Elizabeth Marino

Body Language

after Buñuel & Dali's Un Chien Andalou

In his dreams
     She would find safety beside him,
Would ignore the flash of
     Passing strangers in darkened storefronts.

In his dreams they would
  Go back to her place, turn a single lock
    Enter the plush darkness of her
      Apartment, and he'd easily
       Draw her to him
Without her turning quickly
  To light a small lamp, to glance
    Over and through the clear vinyl shower curtain
And draw the deadbolt, pull the latch and
    Slip closed the chain, giving a slight push
      For good measure.

In his dreams on this warm night
     They'd wander out onto her back porch
       Her face washed in silver by the full moon.
And when he'd stroke her right cheek
     She wouldn't flinch, and when he nuzzled
       The nape of her neck, all that he'd feel
    Would be the soft syllable
      "OH"
    Without the slight stiffening and soft
      "Shit" and sigh.

In his dream
     He could offer her
  Night's endless possibilities
     And she would stroke him
    Till her heart was more than full.

Impossible Before Dante—
An Impotence Poem

*"The supreme misfortune is when
Theory outstrips performance."*
—Notebooks of Leonardo DaVinci

You curl away from me.

Outside
The August sidewalk
Once could fry eggs
Or at least crinkle the air.
Tonight, amber ribbons
Catch the eyes
Of lightening bugs and Johns.

Somewhere, a door
Opens and closes without
Anyone entering.

The air is smooth above us.
I could swear it's winter—
Our words become mist
Then breath again.
How did we go
From children's games
Slipping together as easily as
Into a Chinese finger toy?
We began by baring arms.
I call up the spirit of
Richard Nixon
"Let's de-escalate this war"—
I'm not your
Loving cup.

To the Visitor

He trots past my new place
Hesitates, then approaches
Sniffing the softly drifted snow
On my front stoop. Yes, I am a bitch.
But the season's all wrong
To be in heat.

        He paces
Remembering the faint white scars
Traced with his tongue.
We were both scavengers then;
I had not quite learned to hunt,
He liked the low-life smells.

And now, behind my own door
I'm up to my ears in blood.
My first real prey
Throbs in my mouth.

        Come friend.
Circle my home three times.
Tilt back your shaggy head.
Let us howl in rounds.

Lorraine Mejía-Green

Olive

"Your skin is olive."

"My skin is sap green?"

Green.

"Olive?" a child, I thought,

I am more dull than viridian,
not phthalo,

The color of my shame.

The ad for a cookbook—

with Cristina's
una RUBIA

Prevention Health books en
español

Confesiones irresistibles de
            amante del buen comer

I am not blonde

I AM NOT OLIVE,

no skin the color of snow

not green,

Me—the color of sunshine upon the sand.

Conversation with My Parents in Two Parts

I.
If I could go back as I am now
to when my mother was 25, I'd
tell her what I know now.
I'd tell her that the man (my daddy)
she was about to marry
was a good man
and would make her happy,
but marriage and Minnesota and children and her father
and fear
(yes fear)
would destroy her.
I'd tell her that her in-laws
would call her Aztec (in contempt)
and more
and that she wouldn't forgive them.
She'd hold the venom deep inside (like her father)
and feed the fear of it
to her children, until her husband
turned to God
and her children
elsewhere.
I'd tell her she'd grow more ashamed each year
and mask it under control   craziness
                    craziness   control.

If I could have told her these things, I think
she would have still married my father.

But maybe things would be different now.
Maybe I wouldn't be writing this poem.

II.
If I could go back as I am now
to when my father was 22, I'd
tell him what I know now.
Beware of men in black collars.
Heaven is upon the earth,
only men do not see it.
(You will not see it).

Jennifer Morales

Letter to a Friend's Husband
for Mara

All she is
asking is to hear you say her
name.
She knows her name
but asks you
to speak the four letters
that encircle her idea of self,
to admit to recognition,
to say, "I know you."

Say it,
have it, hold it
in sickness and in health,
in boredom and monotony,
in washing and drying.

Say it
for richer, for poorer,
for slicing and dicing,
for hemming and pressing
'til death.

Do you part your lips to speak
her name silently
at work or nearing sleep
as you once did?

If you could take her name,
where would you go?

Take her name.
Romance it, wine it, dine it.
Set it on her finger like a ring

of remembrance.
Remember
your wife.
Your wife
remembers your name.

Hyperbole

Let's get it straight:
Eskimos do not have 200 words for snow.
They have three, possibly four, which is more
than the average
Joe in the street,
but not more than your median-income skier in Vail.

The number got this high because, like in the children's
game of Telephone, the message became garbled,
from linguistic field research notes,
to academic article, to textbook,
to gown, to town,
to the average Joe in the street.
It grew, swollen with that tingly, vascular feeling
white people get,
that petty awe they feel
for a charming brown people and their ineffable
connection to nature.
And anyway the story
is better like that.

In any attentive heart
a thousand words for snow lie dormant.
One for my father and uncle on a street in Chicago
in drifts up to their grown-man shoulders, photo,
December 1969.

One for the wind-whipped skirts I found

dressing the trees one morning last year
when no one else was around and I was enough
for myself, for once.

Something for a snowball fight with a soon-to-be
ex-lover, when the pelting against my heavy coat
meant something else, meant, "I'm done.
I'm done. I'm done. Let's reduce this love
to ritual violence and go home
apart."

There is a word for snow in our language
and there are words for snow.
"200 words for snow ..." in a disbelieving voice
is a sure ice-breaker at parties, a lot of noise.

Our frozen hearts defy the explanation
or the nomenclature of an objective science.

Control Group

In the Museum of Science and Industry
in a stairwell
you will find cross-sections of human
bodies, several; the sign says they were
homeless
people.
They were
people, and when they died, because nobody
loved them, the state
could freeze them stiff
and slice them into instructive pieces with a chainsaw.

When I was a child I used to come here
with my crazy dad. My crazy dad who
loved me to pieces.

The pieces.

The pieces are pressed
between two long glass windows
and from my knee-high perspective
I could not see then what I see easily today:
these homeless people were black,
you can tell
from the hair because the faces,
well, what did they do with the faces?

At the time,
at the time these people died
black men in Alabama
were succumbing in an informative manner
to syphilis.
It was done for the benefit of all mankind.
Treatment was withheld
to maintain the integrity
of the experiment.

Life, the experiment. Look at the human
body. You can see it here so clearly,
in a different way, of course,
than what you are used to.
But there it all is:
the stomach empty of its yearnings,
no longer the guiding organ
that it was;
the brain with its arroyos drained of thought;
the delicate anus spread out like a pressed flower;
these hands
so quiet now that there is no work to be done.
Who can guess the shame of these windows?
These windows.

The museum officials will not
answer my questions,
so I am waiting for the black homeless,

some ambassadors of justice,
to come reclaim
these bodies,
like the Indians for their pilfered bones
and the Egyptians for their mummies.
When will they come to take back
their dead?
There is no hope of reconstructing
these bodies
on a case-by-case basis
and the faces are lost so
who could recognize them?
They will have to be buried as is:
stack the parts pressed between glass,
dig the hole, cover them,
call it a night,
a night of total darkness.

Goodnight, unloved flesh.
Goodnight. Lights out in the stairwell,
visitors gone home. Where the people
once hung
there are only blue walls
and white spots where the brackets were,
where once hung this strange shame.
Goodnight.

Traveling Light

There was a shoe store clerk.
I met her while shopping for sensible shoes
that I needed for a trip to the islands.
At the time, 17,
I knew that the secret to traveling light
was packing all in one color,
taking only clothes that matched.
The color I chose was blue.

"Comeback," said the shoe store clerk,
"and show me your pictures."
It's not what she was saying
but how she said it that made me
stop a second at the door, turn
and say, "No."

So much later now I see the thing
she saw in me.
At the time, I was 17,
and I was a suitcase hastily closed,
shut on the hem of a dress,
its edges trailing behind for all the world
to see.

Can I go back now and show her my pictures,
still lifes of where I have been?
I am unpacked.
I gave away so many things that didn't fit,
those shoes, those blue clothes. Dead weight.
Ballast to steady a life I don't want to live.

That shoe store clerk, what she saw,
I've taken it out of my suitcase
and put it on,
a fabulous dress
which matches nothing.

Carmen Alicia Murguía

When I Grow Up I Want to Be a Mariachi

When
I
grow up
I want
to be
a Mariachi!
One who
strides
through
La Plaza
surrounded by
guitarras
and
charm
and
harmony
in
a black
wool
charro
outfit
embroidered
in
white silk detail
snake-skin
Tony Lamas
beneath
a sombrero
trimmed
in
gold
with
a velvety-smooth
voice
to match

serenading
women
the songs
they remind me of: Canciones de Amor

When
I
grow up
I want
to
be
a Mariachi!
Because
as it is
right now
my
choices
are limited to
becoming a wife,
a cook,
a mother,
or a lover without a man to depend on.

So, I'm told,
(without revealing my dreams to anyone),
"Seven-year-olds
shouldn't
look
at
other
little classmates,"
the way
I look
at
you
and
want
so much

to serenade you

with
Songs of Love.
"It's not right!" they say.

So, if I must
be
a man
in order
to
experience
your
eyes
watching
my
hands
command
la guitarra,
and
your
body
quivering
every
time
I
cry
out
your name
with
an "A-A-Y-Y-Y!"
and
your
hands,
your hands
applauding
in Spanish...
then,
let's
get on
with
the operation.

Border Crossing

I did not ride in the trunk of a Chevy. I was the driver. I did not need my birth certificate; they knew my name. I did not apply for a Green Card either. I was born here! ¡Nací aquí! I was crossing a different border, that invisible county line de niña a mujer, crossing over from a girl to a woman.

Barbed wire carved beneath my skin as I crawled on my hands into adolescence through the kitchen door and out of the classroom, and on my knees, hoping to find some-one the authorities could not.

Now, how difficult can it be to find a Mexican woman and her poetic child wrapped up in a bold S-A-R-R-R-A-P-E of dreams? I'd find her anywhere only...

I was absorbed by the American flag. Yes, indeed! The good ol' red, white and star-spangled blue wrapped 'round me so tightly—a straight jacket of the English language, baseball, hot dawgs and hot apple pie poured into my veins, turned my skin so pale I slipped right past the bor-der patrol!

You see, this was no ordinary Mexican woman they were looking for. I had a diploma in one hand, a woman on the other, and the keys to MY OWN CHEVY.

Not a trace of blood or tears, not even shame did I leave behind on that dry soil, as I crossed *my* border de niña a mujer.

Ana L. Ortiz de Montellano

The Desk Drawer

Twenty years my friend and teacher, and Toni
caught me by surprise. In black silk and turban,
grande dame of ballet, I could only call her
Antoinette. She deflected our admiring
glances. *It's all done with mirrors.* Precarious
on a rickety table, she sipped water straight
from the clear pitcher. Her child eyes

clung to her replacement's entrechats, cabrioles,
and jetés. Even when they'd cut her rib
so she had to prop one arm with the other
and couldn't demonstrate a port de bras,

her words gestured, *There's a million dollars
between your thighs. Hold them tight. Spiral
those barber pole legs. Grasp the arc above
as you bend.* On her t-shirt, a waif teetered

at a sharp angle off a peak reaching for a star.
A jester's cap replaced her springing curls.
Did she feel like a teenager, grounded?
Her emphasis shifted, *Ground your landing.
Let your breath lead you through the jump.*

I stopped visiting. I couldn't stand
to see in her eyes what, as a child, I'd seen
in my father's eyes. I couldn't stand
before the void. I could only
follow the elder's advice, *When
you look at the coffin, spit.*

Toni came anyway in the night, whispering
that she'd moved to a smaller house. Could she
lock her papers in the drawer of my desk?

No, I didn't want her invasion.

but on Memorial Day when her t-shirts fluttered
across the studio on their hangers, I snatched
the one I loved, the wild-haired woman
with the caption, *Do what terrifies you.*

El Umbral

Far from Teotihuacán
this Solstice, where fifty thousand of my raza
step through el umbral at the top of the pyramid
to the Sun

               the Mississippi swells
into Lake Pepin. A young man, back erect, snakes
up the bluff before me. Gnats shimmer.
Clumps of foliage choke the path.

               Where many feet have left
the earth raw, I slip down a river of pebbles,
grasp at a bush, lurch to the foil-littered
shelf.

               Massive as the bone
white serpent in my dream,
from the flesh of this Lakota
ground arches

               In Yan Teopa
               Teepee Doorway Rock
               Threshold Rock

                 *

My bones are the rock, el umbral.

The chiropractor jolts his hip into my lumbar.
The vertebrae grate in a prolonged quake.

> *The lamps swayed when I was a child,*
> *my bed creaked. Cipactli, the earth*
> *crocodile, rumbled, torn asunder*
> *by four snakes, the old ones said,*
> *so that corn would grow from her body.*

My muscles' habit ropes
the bones back to their strain.

> *Last week on a Minnesota farm a woman*
> *of my raza was shackled and raped,*
> *then set to rake open a corn field.*

Another jolt; the vertebrae release

> *snakes that thrash in the night—*
> *a threshold that parts like the Red Sea*
> *where the white snake of my spine spires up,*
> *its triangular head (we call it sacrum)*
> *pointed down.*

*

I sprinkle water under the arch of In Yan Teopa
in a cross, the ancient cross of sacred corn,
our sustenance.

> *The Bishop of St. Dominic scolded me*
> *for dropping a vial of holy oil.*

With open palm I touch this coil,
one resonant coil along the continental spine,

Umbral	*Threshold*
In Yan Teopa	*Teepee Doorway Rock*
Teotihuacán	*The Place Where One Turns to God*

Reverence

For my father, the author who dreamed me
before I was conceived:

> *Como en la uña de la tierra el pez,*
> *en mi mano germina la figura*
> *de la niña que no supo crecer.*
>
> *Milagro de listón labrado en plata;*
> *gigante es el clavel en la palmera*
> *como la niña que nació en mi palma.*

—Bernardo Ortiz de Montellano, "Primero Sueño," 1931

I am offended by the smell of carrion. Then I see it—
black with white spots or white with black spots.
I'd swear it's a dog, you know, with rather short legs.

It's a cat. I can tell by its delicate head, pointed teeth
in its half open mouth—the only part unaltered by death—
an enormous cat with yellow eyes.

Are they really yellow? I draw near. Maggots swarm
in the opaque sockets. On impulse I scoop up the cat,
drop it. My skin crawls to the elbows like the buzz of flies

on carcass. How to pick it up? With reverence
I hold its two white paws, carry it as if it were
a dancing partner to the patch of grass beside the road.

***

The rust of paper clips spreads on the brittle manuscripts
like fungus. The old Remington's cursive slithers
across loose sheets. The blurred ink of his best friend

Jaime's letters from Madrid reveal an intimacy

I cannot claim. *Me hablas de la inquietud de partir
en que actualmente vives. Te comprendo.*

I wrap the papers in plastic bags labeled Winter Silks,
stack them in reinforced cardboard boxes, and return them
to the poet's wife, my mother, to bury in the airtight

mausoleum of a rare book library.
The cat corpse smolders in a green grave.
The pressed flower notebooks lie in state.

***

I never saw my father
as a corpse to know what a dead man is.
They buried him forty years ago while I

lay in bed, five years old,
bowels a white-knuckled fist
knotted against the dark.

I never saw my father in my dreams
until yesterday when he spoke to me
from behind a stranger's face with the blue eyes.

In my face, only the Zapoteca cheekbones are my father's,
yet I know in the heart of the dream,
este desconocido es mi papá.

Beatriz Reid Dettloff

Tip-toes

Light in the hallway
shining softly
enough to illuminate
design on the carpet
socks on hardwood floor
not enough
to startle me from sleep

Muffled sounds
from the kitchen:
water running
spoon scraping
that old blue bowl
we bought in México
the clink of silver on tile.

These sounds call me,
a diver come up
from the fluid depths,
back to the realm
of the day-to-day.

I reinstate myself in my habitat,
this house that I share
with a man who gets
up before sunrise
and walks softly
so as not to wake me.

Harvesting

Skirt soaked with tomato slop
feet caked with mud that
fills the hollows between my toes
and forms a wet brown arch support,
I pick tomatoes.

I step gingerly among pregnant plants
so heavy with round ripening
they no longer even try
to stand up straight—
they lie, legs spread, to be delivered
of their fruit.

Legions of women before me
have fed families
with this food;
my sisters for centuries
my unknown aunties
lifting these fuzzy stems,
carefully closing their hands
around this smooth red fruit.

I want to invoke them
but I do not know their names.
How did they call themselves?
Anonymous mothers
who have no names in history books,
still I call upon them:

O, nameless women
who for generations have gathered food
from this continent of corn,
this land of squash, of tomatoes and beans,
today I am blest to join you.

I stand in this September sun
my feet anointed in mud

touched with the blood of these tomatoes
I take my place among you:
American women
harvesting.

South Side Post Office Poem

There is no high fashion here.
These are people in vinyl boots
winter jackets zipped up to the chin
men in navy and K-Mart maroon
women in babushkas
and thrift store coats.

Rudy Sutschek, Manager
of the South Side Postal Station,
smiles in bureaucratic benevolence
from a frame of imitation wood
hung on a paneled door.

We stand in line with letters or pick up packages
from California ...México ...San Juan
places where oranges and jasmine bloom.
We are patient folk.
We are Milwaukee in March.
We know how to wait.

Earrings

Hammered crescents of gold
fastened each by a simple hinge:
these I wear in my ears.

Earrings of Tarascan women
who wrap babies in their shawls
hold their children close to them
and walk with daughters to the stream.
Knee-deep mountain water
they bathe in the Sierra Madre sun.

I walk on concrete streets
and dwell with telephones.
Earrings, protect me.

Graciela Reyes

Cada uno el deseo del otro

1.

las zonas libres
de mi cuerpo
las zonas heredadas
las zonas que recuerdan y presienten
son tierra negra húmeda sedosa
con sus gusanos gordos
sus flores amarillas
y absorben tu discurso
como lluvia
y producen
el pan la uva las tardes las semillas

2.

detrás del cristal
la trompa del avión espera
no termina la tarde
creo que nunca terminará esta tarde
ya no somos
lo que éramos
sólo somos
cado uno
el deseo del otro

3.

cuando te diste vuelta
te mostré mis dos manos
levantadas abiertas
quise decirte

que te daba todo
que no cesaría nunca
mi dádiva
levantaste tus manos grandes huesudas
abiertas
y te fuiste.

❧ ❧ ❧

Each One the Other's Desire
Translated by **Jackie White**

1.

the free zones
of my body
the indigenous zones
the zones that remember and intuit
are moist silky black earth
with plump worms
yellow flowers
absorbing your discourse
like rain
and bringing forth
bread grape afternoons seeds

2.

behind the glass
the nose of the plane waits
there is no end to the afternoon
I think that this afternoon will never end
we are no longer
what we were
we are only
each one

the other's desire

3.

when you turned around
I showed you my hands
lifted up opened
I wanted to tell you
that I was giving you everything
that my giving
would never cease
you lifted your huge bony hands
opened them
and took off

Palabra Poema

El poema es siempre
una palabra, una sola palabra,
recortada del silencio. Como un cuchillo
se aguza la luz, y la niña juega
en un claro del parque, rodeada de edificios, calles, y coches,
ella sola en el círculo verde. Un poema
debería ser esa perfecta soledad del parque,
el susurro de los algarrobos, la violenta claridad,
la tierra húmeda amiga que se le mete por las sandalias
y le ensucia los deditos de los pies. Esa soledad,
la vida y el poema, una palabra. Ahora,
sola en mi círculo de luz,
puedo pronunciar esa palabra y repetirla
y creer que el presente
es imborrable.

ॐ ॐ ॐ

Word Poem
Translated by **Jackie White**

Always the poem is
a word, a single word
cut out of silence. Like a knife
the light sharpens, and the little girl plays
in a clearing of the park, surrounded by buildings, streets, and cars,
all alone in the green circle. A poem
ought to be that perfect solitude of the park,
the rustle of locust trees, the violent clarity,
the familiar moist earth that squishes through the sandals
and dirties her little toes. That solitude,
life and the poem, one word. Now,
alone in my circle of light,
I am able to utter that word and repeat it
and think that the present
is indelible.

Silvia Rivera Ramírez

The 3rd Shift

Lying on the naked mattress
hot
sweaty
sticky
like a paleta under the sun.
The air conditioner 'aint working
abanicos blowing muggy air.
Listening to the Polish people
fighting upstairs—
a window breaks,
shuffling feet
racing down the concrete.
Fumbling thoughts
intercepted by alarm clocks.
Daddy's working the third shift—
dim bathroom lights
shadows dancing on the wall
water boiling on the stove
instant coffee
'cause the coffee maker broke.
Infomercials blaring
heavy boots squeaking,
creeping across the linoleum floor
car keys dangling.
"Que Dios te cuide y te bendiga," Mami says.
Heavy bolts
open
close.
Ignition sputters.
Wheels peel away
over shattered glass.
Mami walks into the room, asks,
"¿Mi'ja, estás dormida?"
Breathe in

breathe out
twitching eyelids.
Yes Mami,
I am sleeping.

La Superior

La Superior
back in the hey day
the gateway—
street life
living the best way.
Neglected
children stepping on cracks,
mothers breaking their backs—
black eyes blue.
What to do?
Rabid white dogs
chasing the shorties
down the block—
the bites of life
feeling the pain
of the knife.
Eddie got his
that hot July night
people awoke
to silent screams
heard under cobijas,
bodies lying on the floor
like tortillas.
Playing hopscotch
over calendar days
into alleyways
where Hector
the garbage collector

stayed,
where children prayed
at Holy Innocents,
wore white gloves
on communion Sunday,
played with guns
that next Monday,
bought candy cigarettes
at Ralphie's
for a penny,
blew chalky smoke into the air
before going to school
to D.A.R.E.
smuggling gum into class
hoping to pass.
The 2:30 bell
was greeted by Cobras and Jivers
men carrying their bibles
never realizing
this was survival.

Poster Boy

Looking smooth "chuco,"
Persistent creases in yo' pants.
Órale!
Dig the ruby silk,
Pencil thin mustache,
Shoe-shined shoes.
Well groomed,
Tilted hat,
Suspenders snap.
Zoot up vato!
There's gonna be a riot!

Pilsen

The day washes away in the rain,
the hours spinning at the quickwash
waiting for a free dry.
I step on Aztec time
in search of the Blue Island.
For Sale by owner. By who?
By owner.
César Chávez needs a face lift,
weeds growing out of his neck,
dreams escaping from the cracks,
gasping for sunlight.
I need Sopa de Pollo para el Alma,
or a milagro,
or some Buddha,
Jesús,
or la Virgen María action figures.
Signs advertise "Remedios para cada mal":
a rosary,
some herbs,
incense,
hasta aloe vera to cure all ills.
Dormir, es morir un poco...morir, es despertar.
"A couple of kids got taken down on that block too..."
over there on Laflin,
but nobody's laughing,
just the paper skulls from the upstairs window.
Days of the dead are over, but still alive.
A woman screams,
"Give me back my cigarettes!"
her fist punching innocent raindrops
ricocheting off damp walls.
Burning cardboard boxes smell sweet,
or could it be the bread baking at the panadería?
Steam escapes my mouth,
as I walk,
diligently,
forcefully,

a locomotive lost in the fog
with no destination in sight.
Walking
among pigeons that flock
and bow down to the Loomis eagle,
Tortillerías Sabinas,
Los Milagros,
La Joya,
La Casa Del Pueblo,
Lupe's Beauty Salon,
Café Jumping Bean—
jigsaw puzzles of the night.
These are the streets of my adolescence—
never ending concrete checkered streets
that blurred when I raced down them
into the words on this page.
I've stumbled upon the litter on this floor,
over crumbling cracks,
as I have many times on my cluttered thoughts.
Now I watch as the wax on these windows
flaps in the wind,
"Hello," or perhaps..."Goodbye."

The Housekeeper

Grandma, run! They are expecting you.
Dirty dishes,
Unfed children,
Unkept beds.
Brownie needs to be walked.
Watch out! Men in Green!
Run....Run....Run!
Cross the bridge. Bear its weight.
You made it.
Look back later.
El Paso—follow rugged brick roads.
Jack and Jill wait. They tumble and fall without you.
Make Candyland dreams come true.
When you're done, run!
Dirt floors expect you.
Leave green blurs behind.

Aidé Rodríguez

Green House

In my green house
dark-skinned women wear braids
and ride bright yellow buses.
There are no fences.
The buses weave in and out of banana trees
sprouting in a forest of evergreen pine,
palm, redwood, and baobabs.
The trees grow gradually
beneath the stare of women,
rifles on their laps.

In my green house
there are no free riders, just freedom fighters.
Global warming is something that happens
when my mother dances and sings,
her forehead radiating a most glorious heat.
My brothers and sisters eat and drink together
at one round table,
and greedy men in gray suits
wait on them and wash the dishes
after we have finished feasting on tortillas and beans.

In my green house
the plants are watered by huge Olmec heads,
fountains spitting crystalline
every hour when the flowers change their color.
The walls are windows, murals, of stained glass.

Once

I dreamt of chiseled caves
Carved in the face of Jesus and saints,
Ancient Mexica figures and codex symbols,
Glazed by water spilling.

I walked through a door into
A red carpeted casino, lights stinging
And slot machines ringing, loud.

Clouds formed an angel
Behind the horizon of some dark sea.
The Virgen Mary floated like a buoy,
A white oval statue.

When she reached the angel's grasp
Lightening struck and thunder roared.
The clouds drifted apart, and fast,
Two tornados made their way toward
The beach where I was watching
My family's picnic,
And a metallic house that gleamed.

I climbed a mountain where
A circle of men and one woman,
Dark and round, were sitting.
She braided my hair.

We

Walk in fine night
Shadow world
Serpents leaving traces on silky desert sand
Our mother's belly

Climbing icy hills
Grasping frozen branches
Moon reflected on winter's leaf

Sliding down muddy jungles
Rain forest heat
Tripping over ancient roots
Ends buried too deep for us to see

Treading the cycle of time
Bearing the burden of history
Hard concrete beneath our feet

We walk in fine night
Descendents of those who knew
How to read the earth's secrets
Hidden stars scatter across black sky
Draping just above our heads

You Sober Princess

You wear velvet shirts.
Their sleeves end at elegant elbows
Smelling of opium
And other costly scents—
Sharpie markers,
Turpentine, pain thinner.
Wipe the mismatched colors from your canvas.
Lie on plush blue couches.
Drink wine from royal glasses.

What will you do with yourself?
Have a child, baby prophet
Name him Jesús
After a dead uncle?
Marry a rich man
Who needs a colorful ornament on his arm?
Live in a four bedroom house—
Forty acres and a mule?

Will you write songs?
Get orchids thrown at your naked feet?
Haunt nameless faceless men?
Wear nail polish that sparkles like cosmic sky—
Sunbelt wrapped around your waist?

Will you hide in a room
Made of dried earthen bricks?
Watch the rain
Drip fast for days
Destroying everything into the sea?

Nydia Rojas

Routine

"Me gusta lavar la ropa. Me ayuda a pasar el día."
"I like doing the laundry. It helps me get through the day."

—Guatemalan woman in a shelter after hurricane Mitch devastated her country.
November, 1998

She takes
the paper cup full of water
to her lips,

savors the liquid's coolness
as her tongue slowly
awakes to the clean taste.

To her back, she hears the morning
breeze. The change of clothing she washed earlier
flaps on the clothesline.

Tomorrow, she'll go through
it again: One pail of water
to wash the family clothes.

Then she'll hang them
on the clothesline stretching between
a surviving tree and the building

housing the displaced families.
Task accomplished, she'll walk
to the line

of orange and red
plastic barrels and ask for
a glass of water.

She'll drink it in small
sips, feel the tingling

sensation on her tongue

sending a wake up call
to the rest of the body.
For now, only her hands
respond. The change of clothes
must be dry by the
following morning.

As her hands
scrub blouses and skirts,
shirts and pants

she studies the
river's water slowly
receding.

Redefining First Names

Somebody validates my whole existence
by explaining to me I am now a minority.

I am baffled.

I have always thought of myself
as the name my first grade teacher
taught me to spell, first letter always capitalized.

Something unlike a plant or a vegetable
or a rock. Something not so generic.

That someone even spells the word
minority for me. His eyes speak
of knowledge, so I believe he's
telling me the truth.

The smell of hills and salty sea water
still lingers on my dress, my hair,
my skin. It must be true.

My lazy tongue retracts, falls silent,
trying to reconstruct these sounds
to which it can not mold itself.

It must be true. Those eyes of wisdom,
baptizing me with freezing rain and foreign
rituals, exercising their right
to claim my name on the grounds of their knowledge.

I slip between the letters. In and out.
In and out. A busy spider knitting
a web around me from within which
I will redefine the word *minority*.

A golden thread shimmers
in the dark, leads me through the maze.

I redefine the wisdom of those eyes
taking away my name.

Rice

"You'll need three cups of water.
The grains grow bigger after
they've cooked." She poured
the water on the heavy, iron pot,
carefully measured a cup and a half of rice.
"This is enough to feed nine people.
Then add some salt." She reached
for the round container with the little
girl smiling under the umbrella.

Unlike my mother, I always took my time
adding salt to the boiling water.
I studied the cardboard tub, wondered
what adventures hid behind the umbrella.

After my mother casually mentioned
that salt came from the sea, I thought
of pirates trying to steal our salt and rice.

The sweet, starchy fragrance filled
the air as the water boiled away.
The red, blue and yellow plates rested
on the open shelves lining the kitchen wall.

"You need to occasionally stir it," and her wrist
masterfully inserted the spoon all the way to the
bottom of the pot and brought up the rice—softer
and tender—which had been closer to the heat.

This step always left me exhausted.
The spoon refused to go as deep
when guided by my inexperienced hands.

The plates paraded through the kitchen—
one child at the time. There was no space
for more. The rice became white mounds
surrounded by a red, blue or yellow frame.

Then we sat on whichever chair was empty
and ate—sometimes quietly;
sometimes my mother's stern look
reminded us we were being too noisy.

Most times, we just sat down and ate.

Blank Wall

Chalk in hand she scribbles
words every which way they fit.
There's no time for concessions
to space or right spelling.

mountains as tall as the stars
on nights of new moon

After the rain, colorful drops
of water slide from one word to the next.

Every rainy day leaves behind a blank wall
to be filled while the churn of the washing machine
fills her early morning hours.

She wants to rescue her voice
but the rain is always stronger
and leaves behind only blue
and red puddles covering the cement floor.

blackbirds marking distances
with their extended wings

She learns about the temporality of her days.
She knows time cannot be filled with words—
not even the ones briefly decorating the blank wall.

She discovers why the clean clothes
flap on the line: they had dreamed
they were birds whose wings had been clipped.

Chalk in hand she pretends
that her hand is not guided
by old spirits reclaiming their voices.

house four walls a roof and a window
to let the light shine on the particles
of levitating dust.

Irasema Salinas

Coahuila Prayers

I.
I hear the bebito cry.
Let it all out, I say.
Learn to extinguish the pain.
Learn to smother the anger.

I hear the niño laugh.
Devour the joy, I say.
Learn to laugh 'til your dizzy.
Learn to laugh 'til your delightfully numb.

And then I will tell you what
I hear in my America.
And like me you will see
how crucial it is to cry and laugh.

II.
I hear La Raza's Prayers,
we invoke Guadalupe.
I hear my Mother's prayers,
she invokes the Holy Spirit.
I hear my Father's prayers,
he invokes Jehovah.
I hear pre-Colombian Gods call,
they invoke me.
I long to find them, touch the toes of my roots.

I hear my bisabuela's presence; she hints about my past.
I hear unoccupied Coahuila.
I hear colonized Coahuila.
I hear the mines exploding in Coahuila.
I hear her call me to the monte, to return to the Coahuila tribe.
I hear her mourn Manifest Destiny's fate.

III.
I hear the heavy pesos fall from your pockets.
I hear you climbing a fence.
I hear you swimming in el Río Grande.
I hear America threatening me,
I defy her and help you.
Because I hear voices that tell me,
originally the Earth was meant to have no borders.

IV.
I hear the stiff joints of tired mothers.
I hear the insistent tug of the conveyor belt.

I hear the loud wail of a stunned father
who dozed because life got sleepy.
He's lost his four right fingers.
I hear the cardboard crash.
There's a jam, the code blue is in effect.
Someone call the constipated nurse.

I hear you ask him,
"¿Qué vas hacer ahora?"
I hear the mayordomo,
"This is America, speak English."

V.
I hear the paletero's chimes.
I hear you beg your ma,
"I wanna paleta! I wanna paleta!"

I hear the whining braids of the columpios.
Higher, higher but my feet never touch the clouds.

I hear the Nikes skidding about the court.
I hear the orange ball bounce, bounce, bounce.

I hear the trumpets blaring

On the Banda lovers radio.
This vaquero means business
in his 4x4, black Dodge Ram pick-up.

I hear Little Suzy begging for a hug.
Riding in a borrowed Chrysler, these girls are heavy duty;
black liquid liner, thick mascara, and dark plum lips.
Their roots exposed, they're heading
for the Nice & Easy sale.

I hear the hypnotic base, it's the house tape.
He's a block away, cruisin' by himself
in the financed Buick.
The overtime has helped him buy
the rims, the amp, and the Kenwood,
volume as high as he's cravin' to be.

I hear the lost rhymes,
one surviving speaker In the Ford.
It's the shabby boy in black taken aback
by the Rock en Español tape his novia made for him.

I hear a whistle drunk and flushed.
I hear a response,
"Tu madre, cabrón."

It's a summer symphony.

VI.
I hear they taught you the alphabet.
I hear they forgot to teach you how to count.
I hear they taught you how to spell your name.
I hear they forgot to teach you how to add.
I hear they taught you how to write your name.
I hear they forgot to call on you.
I hear they taught you how to sign, sign, sign, your life away.
They forgot to teach you how to read.

VII.
I hear the conflict.

I hear the bullet breaking skin.
I heard it crack your skull.

I hear the wailing sirenas.
I hear you gasp for life.
I heard you sneak away.

VIII.
I have no love poem for America.
I don't share Whitman's romance.
I sympathize with Ginsberg.

I face tomorrow,
I listen,
And I hear the Coahuila prayers.

The Maid's Daughter

The maid's daughter licks
her fingers when she eats Doritos.
Carries her toys in a
plastic thrift-store bag.

The maid's daughter visits every Saturday
helps her mother
wash clothes
and make beds.
She wants to play
with your three Cabbage Patch dolls
but is never allowed.

The maid's daughter realizes
your mother,
adored by your father,
is jealous of the maid.

The maid's daughter resents
your sloppy rooms
your hand-me-downs
your disapproval.

The maid's daughter hates
the long rides to your house
She feels ashamed,
     awkward,
       clumsy in your presence.

The maid's daughter takes comfort
knowing that at least the maid never
sold-out like your mother.

Contradictions

I will no longer deny it,
I am a feminist with contradictions.

I was once called a dyke
'cause I refused to wear my hair
like a virgin veil.
But it was at a man's request
that I allowed my head
to birth an ebony waterfall.

I rejected the broom
that used to tip-toe
past my bedroom door.
But I was the one who fell
three paces back
and, with a wet mop,
cleared the muddy trail left
by his grimy steel-toed work boots.

I inherited my father's indecision.
I am his female counterpart.

My father,
un macho mexicano,
resented the working woman
he married.
All the while he puzzled me
with his advice.
He said,
"Go to school,
estudia mucho,
so you can get a good job."

Leda Schiavo

Necesidad y urgencia del viaje

A veces uno no sabe
quién es tú, yo o el otro.
A veces no sé si Ulises soy yo
o si tú eres Ulises
o si yo soy yo, el otro, la otra, o la madre que nos parió.

Ulises, quién nos librará del llamado del mar
del cabrilleo del mar
la mer, la mer, toujours recommencée
del deseo de la tormenta y el estremecimiento siempre
nuevo de los límites.

Astuto Ulises,
a todos nos engañaste durante siglos y Poseidón
nunca se imaginó que tus desplantes
eran uno más de tus ardides.
También él entró en tu mentira y te
arrastró a lo loco por nuestro mar
cómplice involuntario de tu manía ambulatoria.

Quién quiere quedarse toda la vida
en la misma cama matrimonial
ver la misma cara, oir las mismas idioteces
estar siempre con la misma Penélope cuando
el mar espera, la nave se impacienta, las aventuras acechan,
los amores acucian.

Vamos, Ulises, sigamos puteando a Poseidón para
que no nos deje volver y podamos huir
hacia adelante buscando
sirenas de verdad
peligros auténticos, lenguajes
que nunca entenderemos.
Dejemos que los pretendientes se enfurezcan

mientras se beben tu vino
que Telémaco sabrá ocuparse de ellos.

Itaca está siempre ahí pero nosotros seguiremos adelante porque
nuestra patria es el viaje
nuestro destino es el viage
nuestro único deseo es el viaje
navigare necesse
                    vivere non necesse
mejor morir con las sirenas que en los brazos de la costumbre
la costumbre mata lentamente
es como un cáncer que nos va invadiendo
crece como los helechos tropicales
y un día nos deja exánimes en húmedos y letales dormitorios
blandos y entregados al lugar definitivo.
Ubi sunt qui sunt?
No, no, aquí están los que pefieren no estar.

൸ ൸ ൸

Need and Urgency for Travel
Translated by John Fritz

At times one doesn't know
who you are, who I am, or who the other is.
At times I don't know if I am Ulysses
or if you are Ulysses
or if I am me, someone else, or the mother that bore us.

Ulysses, who will deliver us from the call of the sea
from the white-capped sea
la mer, la mer toujours recommencée
from the yearning for the tempest
and the ever new shudder of limits.

Crafty Ulysses
you deceived us all for centuries and Poseidon

never imagined that your impertinence
were but another of your stratagems.
He fell in with your deception as well and
hauled you crazily about our sea
an unwilling accomplice to your ambulatory obsession.

Who wishes to stay forever in the same marriage bed
to behold the same face, to hear the same lunacies
to be forever with the same Penelope when
the sea awaits, the bark waxes impatient,
adventures urge, love arises.

Let us go Ulysses, let us be steadfast in importuning Poseidon
and perhaps he does not permit us to come back and we may
flee onward in search of flesh and blood sirens
authentic dangers, languages
which we shall never understand.
Let us warrant the suitors anger
while they drink your wine
for Telemachus does know how to handle them.

Ithaca is always there but we will continue on because
our homeland is the voyage
our destiny is the voyage
our longing is the voyage
navigare necesse
                    vivere non necesse
better to die with the sirens than in the embrace of convention
habit kills slowly
it is like a cancer that silently invades us
it grows like tropical ferns
and one day leaves us lifeless in damp and lethal dormitories
lax and resigned to the final resting place
Ubi sunt qui sunt?
No, no, here are found those who prefer not to be here.

Ser o no ser

Yo odio sin paliativos a las señoras decentes
que no dudan de nada
que saben de mentiras y formalidades y no las confunden
jamás
porque son sabias de eterna sabiduría
hijas de Eva que han probado la fruta del bien y del mal
y ejercen uno y otro
sin esfuerzo
alternativo y deportivamente.

అ అ అ

Being or Not Being
Translated by **John Fritz**

I loathe without mitigation those flourishing ladies
Who doubt not
Who fathom deceits and certainties and don't confuse them ever
Because they are oracles of eternal sagacity
Daughters of Eve who have tasted the fruit of good and evil
And who practice the one and the other
Effortlessly
Willfully and unerringly.

Maneras de zarpar

1. Me quiero ir, me quiero ir, dijo
   agarrándose a la puerta con desesperación.

2. Oh, sí, el mar, el mar
   el brillo del horizonte
   los rieles de la luna.

3. El deseo de navegar por tus interiores
   las desganadas ganas del empezar.

4. El mar, que recomienza siempre, como mi amor.

5. La lejanía está aquí, la llevo dentro.

6. Sé que no es fácil
   pero quiero estar y no estar
   al mismo tiempo, y bajo el mismo respecto.

7. Aunque sepa los caminos
   yo nunca llegaré a tiempo.

8. Dame la biblia, dame el reloj
   dame tu boca
   dame los zapatitos blancos
   tengo que irme, tengo que verte.
   Me esperas allá abajo, me tirarás de las orejas
   me escucharás, por fin.

9. Volver, volver.
   Ojalá todo esté igual pero mejor
   que me digas alguna vez
   Ulises, volvé, ésta es tu casa,
   te queremos de veras, no importa cómo
   qué, cuál, quién, cúyo, dónde, cuándo.

10. -El tren sale a las tres.
    -También puedo tomar el avión a las cinco.

-Pero a las siete sale el autobús directo.
-Mejor el tren de medianoche. En cuatro horas estás allá.

11. Entre el aquí y el allí, cuánta esperanza y cuánto desasosiego.

12. Y entonces, levó el ancla, arrió las velas
puso el motor a toda marcha
y entró la marcha atrás.

13. Estás allá y mi espacio se duplica;
estás aquí y el espacio se hace denso.

14. Tu cuerpo es el tiempo, horadado de polvo.

ᖇ ᖇ ᖇ

Ways of Setting Sail
Translated by **Beatriz Badikian-Gartler**

1. I want to leave, I want to leave, she cried
while holding desperately onto the door.

2. Oh, yes, the sea, the sea
the brightness of the horizon
the rails of the moon.

3. My longing to navigate through your inner universe
the half-hearted willingness to begin.

4. The sea, which always begins anew, like my heart.

5. Distance is here, I carry it inside me.

6. I know it isn't easy
but I want to be and not to be
at the same time and in the same place.

7. Although I know the way
   I'll never arrive on time.

8. Hand me the Bible, hand me the clock
   give me your mouth
   give me the tiny white shoes
   I have to leave, I have to see you.
   You wait for me down there, you'll pull my ears
   you'll listen to me, at last.

9. To return, to return
   I hope everything is the same but better
   that sometime you will say to me:
   "Ulysses, come back, this is your home.
   We really love you; it doesn't matter how,
   what, which one, who, where, when."

10. The train departs at three.
    -I can also take the five o'clock plane.
    -But at seven the non-stop bus departs.
    -The midnight train is better. You'll be there in four hours.

11. Between here and there, how much hope,
    how much uneasiness.

12. And then she weighed anchor, lowered the sails
    set the motor at full speed
    and pulled the lever backwards.

13. You are there and my space grows double;
    you are here and my space grows dense.

14. Your body is time bored through by dust.

Claudia Rosa Silva

El Hombre Araña

From the 45th floor
of a downtown
condominium high-rise,

I'm startled as I look out the window—

> a bright blue sky,
> Lakeshore Drive
> and the John Hancock building
> in the background—

and make eye-contact
with a seemingly fearless
Spiderman,

a paisano
holding onto a rope,
cleaning my windows from the outside,
making me see
things
a little clearer.

Branded

We were the marked ones, forced to sit
apart from the rest,
the low level kids with "special needs."
Each day at 10:00 in the middle of reading,
an assistant clerk would come to take us away—
four of us.

Joe: the quiet immigrant from Yugoslavia
who spoke and read English well
and had a cute older brother;
Troy: Joe's best friend,
the tan kid whose last name ended in ski,
a Polish-Mexican-American
who spoke neither language and was a slow reader;
Jill: the girl who dressed in ESPRIT,
had short hair like me,
but skin a pale shade of white;
Claudia: There I was, brown
with dark, unshaven legs,
often confused for a boy,
a shy, Mexican niña.

Troy and Joe would mimic a TV jingle
that a black actor declared with a promising grin,
"S-U-C-C-E-S-S, Success!"—
another 80's spiel for some trade school.
I always hoped to leave St. Jude's,
become the next featured student
on DeVry Tech's commercials.

With the assistant, we'd enter a dark, narrow room,
sit in small chairs at a miniature table and read stories,
all of which we had long grown past.
Taking turns to read sentences, some of us stumbled,
praying under our breaths, helped each other,
while the frustrated clerk yelled at us.

Jill read the worst, having a hard time
pronouncing her words.
I would wait to be called on,
counting ahead, hoping for a long paragraph,
dreading mistakes,
trying to enunciate clearly.
Maybe they'd switch me,
place me with "normal," Brady Bunch children.

Oh yes, someday Claudia would be worthy of dignity,
for despite
her Aztlán roots,
unwanted "alien" parents,
Spanish-speaking familia,
she was a good reader.

Entre las gorditas de res, los taquitos de lengua, y los licuados de fresa...

The day we sat eating at Las Gorditas Aguascalientes,
Papi said I could be an eagle!
¡Yo tengo que ser un águila!
¡Yo puedo serlo!

"¿Sabes que hacen las águilas cuando llueve, mi'ja?
Ellas no se esconden como otros;
ellas vuelan con la tormenta,
no tienen miedo."

Okay Papi, está bien. Seré tu águila.
Te dejaré que vueles con mis alas,
seré el beisbolista que siempre soñaste ser,
seré el hijo que nunca tuviste,
seré tu orgullo.

Iremos juntos por un cielo abundante
donde nadie más nos niegue.
Allí, volaremos
con todas las otras águilas
de nuestra bandera.

ॐ ॐ ॐ

Entre las gorditas de res, los taquitos de lengua, y los licuados de fresa...

The day we sat eating at Las Gorditas Aguascalientes,
Papi said I could be an eagle!
I have to be...I can be an eagle!

"Do you know what eagles do when it rains, mi'ja?
They do not hide as others do;
they continue to fly despite the storm,
fearless."

Okay Papi, fine. I will be your eagle,
letting you fly with my wings.
I will be the baseball player you always
dreamed of becoming,
the son you never had,
your pride.

We will go together through an abundant sky
where no one else will ever deny us.
There, we shall fly
alongside all of the other eagles
of our flag.

Johanny Vázquez Paz

Liviana

Quisiera ser liviana como tú
perderme en el deseo de mi cuerpo
sintiendo ansia y lujuria
y poder mirar de frente al siguiente día
los ojos de las bocas extranjeras
que desgusté gozosa sin amor.

Quisiera ser liviana y flotar
sin más preocupación
que mis necesidades
deleitarme como tú gozas
un cuerpo nuevo cada noche
en tus ancianas manos.

Pero soy pesada y me atan
las historias de mi abuela,
los consejos de mi madre,
el orgullo de mi hermana.

¡Cómo han cambiado los tiempos!
Ayer yo era moderna y liberada
hoy sólo niña consentida
de ideas anticuadas.

Y de verdad que quisiera ser
aire ingrávido no contaminado,
espuma flotando en la ola,
rocío resbalando en la hoja.

Pero soy pesada montaña
cargada de raíces e historia
atada a los prejuicios de mi abuela,
a las creencias de mi madre,
a la experiencia de mi hermana.
Quisiera ser liviana como tú,
enséñame a engañar mi alma.

Light Heart
Translated by **Tony del Valle**

I want to be as lighthearted as you are
lose myself in the desire of my flesh
feeling only anxiety and lust
and boldly face the next day
the eyes of the stranger's mouths
sampled in pleasure without love.

I want to be lighthearted and float
without any more care than my needs
luxuriate the way you delight
with a new being each night
in your weathered hands.

But I am heavy and I am bound
by my grandmother's stories,
my mother's admonitions,
my sister's pride.

How times have changed!
Yesterday I was modern and liberated.
Today only a prissy girl
with antiquated ideas!

And in truth I wish I could be
pure, uncontaminated air,
foam floating on the wave,
dew slipping off the leaf.

But I am a heavy mountain
burdened with roots and history
bound to my grandmother's prejudices,
to my mother's beliefs,
to my sister's experience.

I wish to be lighthearted like you,
teach me to deceive my soul.

Por un hilo

Amigo mío,
en estas mis últimas horas de locura inexorable,
quiero que sepas que no existo así como existes tú
o existen mis vecinos y sus amigos
planeando cada noche la rutina del próximo día,
escogiendo en la mañana la ropa que mejor les sienta,
soñando dos semanas de libertad al año
mientras imaginan despiertos sus fantasías y metas.

Yo, por el contrario, no existo, sobrevivo...

por las noches mis ojos evitan la amargura de soñar
y abiertos contemplan soledades
hasta que la mañana llega en emboscada
husmeando los recuerdos que sobraron en la cena;
me paro aturdida frente al ropero y no encuentro que ponerme
nada me sirve, nada me sienta, nada me apetece,
acróbata agarrada de un sólo dedo a la cuerda
sabiendo que al final no habrá malla que me salve,
espero la caída despierta.

Perdidos ya todos los sueños, fantasías y metas
de la memoria de aquella que fui hace algún tiempo
cuando existía como existes tú y mis vecinos y sus amigos
y la vida no era esta búsqueda de aire entre las grietas
para sobrevivir sin soltar el dedo de la cuerda...

෴ ෴ ෴

By a Thread
Translated by **Johanny Vázquez Paz** and **Brenda Cárdenas**

Dear friend,
In these, my last hours of inexorable insanity
I want you to know that I do not exist the same way you
or my neighbors and their friends do,
planning each night, their next day routines,
choosing in the morning the clothes they look best in,
dreaming about two weeks of freedom a year
while imagining their goals and fantasies.

I, on the other hand, do not exist, I survive...

at night my eyes avoid the bitterness of dreams
and openly gaze at wilderness
until the morning comes like an ambush
prying into the leftover memories from dinner;
I stand confused in front of the closet and can't find what to wear.
Nothing fits me, nothing looks good, nothing appeals to me;
an acrobat holding by only a finger to the rope
knowing that at the end there will not be a net to save me,
I wait for the near fall awake.

All the dreams, fantasies and goals already lost
from the memory of the one I was some time ago
when I existed like you and my neighbors and their friends
and life was not this search for air between the cracks
to survive without letting my finger go from the rope.

A la vida

Mi madre me parió con fuerza
me recogió del suelo
y limpió la tierra escondida
entre los caminos
arrugados de mi piel
contó mis dedos
y colgó en mi cuello
un collar de llaves
luego me entregó a la vida
y en el oído
un acertijo marcó mis días:
el mundo es una dicotomía,
escoge el lado de menos grietas
y vive a prisa,
la vida es un minuto
de segundos furtivos.

❧ ❧ ❧

To life

My mother gave birth to me with strength,
picked me up from the ground
and cleaned the hidden soil
between the wrinkled paths of my skin,
counted my fingers
and hung around my neck
a necklace full of keys.
Then she gave me to life
and whispered in my ear
a riddle that marked my days:
the world is a dichotomy;
choose the side with fewer cracks
and live with urgency.
Life is a minute
of furtive seconds.

Morning After

The wind enters quickly through the window
pushing the curtain out of its way
just to touch our backs facing different directions.

With no rehearsal you move closer to me
and I harmonize my curves to your edges
like two connecting pieces from a puzzle.

There is no love to talk about,
this is just the first morning after
but, to our surprise,
the room is covered with tenderness
from your lips calming my fears,
from my fingertips healing your sorrow.

This time I won't dwell in the future.
Always trying to anticipate a lifetime
steals seconds of these few minutes of happiness.

The cool wind doesn't scare
two lonely strangers
that can embrace a tender body
the morning after many mornings
of shivering with only memories to embrace.

Teresa Vázquez

Sin Querer / Queriendo

Lo que no se dice
Lo que no se puede decir
Lo que no vale la pena
Los deseos que se aguantan

Cuando uno no tiene palabras
Para donde la imaginación logra llegar

La vista gorda
La mano grande
Los mangos bajitos
Como el que no quiere las cosas

Sin querer, queriendo
A veces, sí es fácil
Estar parada
En la senda del peligro.

தை தை தை

Without Love / Wanting

What is not said
What cannot be said
What's not worth the trouble—
Reigned desires

When one has no words to describe
The place where imagination has succeeded in taking you

The averted glance
The big hand
Easy fruit
Eaten like someone who didn't want it

Without meaning to, wanting
Yes, sometimes it is easy
To stand
In the path of danger.

Dionisio y Yemayá

La marea casi nunca moja la viña
Pero mojándose con el mar
El sabor de la sal alborota la boca
Al saborear la agridulce fruta
Y con mi boca
Pruebo el sabor
De tu pecho
Adornado con semillas de uvas—
Tus pesones morados y tiernos.

Encima de ti cae mi cabello
Salpicante y profundamente ondeado
Me aseguras que mis greñas no son víboras hambrientas
Sino viñas maduras, enlazadas.

Remueves con tu lengua una gota de calor líquido
Una semilla de sudor
Que ha caído en mi clavícula
Y te digo al oído que entre mis piernas
Te mojaría el mar con gusto
Sin ahogarte, inspirando antojo
Y deseos de beber
Y tú atreviéndote
Empiezas a estudiar
Ese sabor...

O, dios del hambre
Tu hijo, bien bebido
Es mi amante
Añoro el día que lo emborrache.

Dionysius and Yemayá

The tide rarely washes the vineyard
But when the ocean makes it wet
Its salty taste arouses the mouth
That savors the soursweet fruit
And with my mouth
I try the taste
Of your chest
Adorned with grapeseeds—
Your nipples, tender and purple.

Over you my hair breaks
Splashing and deeply wavy
You assure me that my locks are not hungry vipers
But instead mature vines, intertwined.

You remove with your mouth a drop of liquid heat
A seed of sweat
That has fallen on my collarbone
And I whisper, "between my legs
The sea would happily make you wet
Without drowning you, inspiring craving
And the desire to drink,"
And you dare
To study that taste...

O, god of hunger
Your quenched son
Is my lover
I yearn for the day I make him drunk.

The Line

There is a line
but no map—
one just knows.

The line allows you to have
nothing but faith and thanks

The rest is what you harvest
intuiting the line.

The line lets you go
for years at a time

You can visit places that look
like the line

But you will have only souvenirs
when you return.

The line is your mind and your footsteps
finding your heart without trying,

Serendipity is the child
of the line,

Words spoken in thanks-giving
are made of the breath that etches the line,

Fate masquerades as the line
but will be sought out as an impostor,

Faith is a compass, but don't forget
there is no map.

The line does not die;
it is there to be found

in each moment, each word
and each choice.

The line does not judge
or make excuses

The line has its origin in the infinite
and is yours to keep
finding.

Contributors' Notes

Denia Alvarado migrated to the U.S. in 1963 from Costa Rica. Her parents settled in one of Milwaukee's 90 percent German neighborhoods. She says, "Much of my writing comes from experiencing life on the sidelines." Alvarado holds a B.A. in Communications and is working on her M.A. in English at the University of Wisconsin-Milwaukee.

Beatriz Badikian-Gartler was born and reared in Buenos Aires, Argentina, and has lived in the Chicago area for the last thirty years. Badikian-Gartler holds a Ph.D. in English from the University of Illinois at Chicago and teaches writing and literature at Roosevelt University. Her work has been published in numerous journals, anthologies, and newspapers in the U.S. and abroad. Her second full length collection *Mapmaker Revisited: New and Selected Poems* was published by Gladsome Books in 2000.

Sonia Báez-Hernández was born in the Dominican Republic and emigrated to Puerto Rico in 1965. She is both a visual and performance artist who has exhibited her work at the Museum of Modern Art in the Dominican Republic, the Printmaking Society in Los Angeles, and Gallery 2 in Chicago, among others. She holds an M.F.A. from the School of the Art Institute of Chicago, an M.A. in Sociology from the University of California-Los Angeles, and a B.A. in Political Science from the University of Puerto Rico.

Marta Collazo (Pluma) is a Puerto Rican woman born and raised in Lorain, Ohio. She has lived in the Chicago area for the last thirty years. Collazo studied Communications and Literature at the University of Illinois at Chicago. She is a social activist, a mother, an educator, an athlete, and a poet. She has performed her poetry at several venues throughout Chicago.

Daisy Cubias was born in El Salvador and came to the U.S. in 1966. Her work has been published in *I Didn't Know There Were Latinos in Wisconsin* and the *Wisconsin Poets Calendar 2000*. She is co-author of *Journey of The Sparrows* (Dell), a book for young adults, which won the Jane Adams International Women for Peace and Freedom award. It has been translated into Spanish and German and adapted to the theatre in Chicago. She has also published a chapbook, *Children of War*. Cubias has conducted poetry workshops and public readings in Wisconsin, New York, and Nicaragua.

Silvia Divinetz is an Argentinian physician with a small private practice in Minneapolis. She writes in both Spanish and English and has been translating Neruda's poetry. Divinetz's poems have been published or are forthcoming in *Poetry Motel, Nimrod, 100 Words*, and the American Psychiatric Association's 1998 book *Caring for Victims of Torture*.

Venessa Maria Fuentes' home has always been in Minneapolis/St. Paul except for the year she lived in Chicago. She graduated in 1997 from Macalester College with a B.A. in Women's and Gender Studies. Fuentes' poems have been published in *The Gazelle Poets Anthology*, Vol. I and *Swerve* Magazine. She is currently on staff at the Loft Literary Center.

Rina García has a B.A. in Elementary Education and is working toward her M.A. in Literature. Her poems have been published in *Infinite Divisions: An Anthology of Chicana Literature* and by the Poets International Society. She currently teaches in Kankakee, Illinois.

Juana Goergen is from Puerto Rico. She is an Associate Professor of Latin American Literature and Director of Latin American and Latino Studies at DePaul University in Chicago. She has published two books of literary scholarship and a collection of poems: *La sal de las brujas / Witches of Salt*, 1995 (Finalist, Letras de Oro National Contest). Goergen has also published poems in literary journals, such as *Abrapalabra, Tropel* and *Tameme,* among others, and in several anthologies, including *Astillas de luz/Shards of Light* (Tía Chucha Press, 1998).

Lisa Guedea Carreño is a corporate librarian. The January 1999 issue of *Inc.* magazine featured her work as a strategic information specialist in a cover story entitled "The Smartest Little Company in America." Her published works include book reviews, technical articles, professional commentaries and personal essays. Born in Chicago, Guedea Carreño has also lived in Denver, Texas, Kansas, New Hampshire, and Wisconsin. She currently resides in Indiana.

Cristina Herrera was born in Bogotá, Colombia. With a vocation as an aspiring Moyolnonotzani, she is a simmering blend of image-maker, dream-listener, garden-dancer, and word-weaver. Herrera has an Associate Degree in Film-making and engages in ongoing experimentation in hand-made (and bound) miniature books. She has published two chapbooks *The Power to Dream* and *Manos de Seda/Hands of Silk* and a one-poem book *Time Flows in All Directions*. She has also published poems in various periodicals and anthologies.

Ixtaccíhuatl is a Mexican born, U.S. raised poet who has lived in the Chicago area most of her life. She holds a Master's degree from the University of Illinois at Chicago and teaches English. Ixtaccíhuatl's work has appeared in *Another Chicago Magazine, Howling Dog, Hammers, Blue Mesa Review, Sierra Nevada College Review*, and other journals. Her work was nominated for a Pushcart Prize.

Lorena Rosalia Manzo is an actress, poet, graphic designer and entrepreneur. She is co-owner of Bohemian Communications and Apocalypse Entertainment. Manzo holds a B.A. from Columbia College and, in 1998, published a collection of erotic poetry entitled *Sin*.

Janessa María-Diego writes and teaches in Milwaukee. Her voice is *una herencia* from the village of Montefrío,

Andalucía, España. María-Diego's poems have been published in the anthology *Sparkle, Sizzle, Hiss* and in local magazines, such as *Poet's Monday Grab-Bag* and *Tacones lejanos (High Heels)*. She has work forthcoming in *Cream City Review*.

Elizabeth Marino is a Chicago-born Puerto Rican raised in a working class Italian and German family. In addition to writing, she also acts and directs under the name Micaela Mastierra. Marino holds an M.A. in English from the Writer's Program at the University of Illinois at Chicago. Her poems have been published in *Lucky Star, Strong Coffee, Envisage* (UK), *Breaking Mirrors Anthology*, and *Nit & Wit*. Her articles have been published in the *Chicago Journal*, among others.

Lorraine Mejía-Green was born and raised in Minnesota by a Mexican mother and a German American father. She holds a B.A. in Sociology and is working toward her M.F.A. in Writing. Mejía-Green was a 1998 winner of the Loft's Chicano Latino Inroads Program for Emerging Writers. Her poems have been published in the College of St. Benedict's *Diotima* and *The Catholic Spirit* of the Archdiocese of St. Paul and Minneapolis.

María Dolores Mercado earned her B.A. from the National School of Painting, Sculpture and Printing "La Esmeralda" of the National Institute of Fine Arts in México, D.F. She is currently a Museum Arts Educator at the Mexican Fine Arts Center Museum in Chicago and host of *Camino Tierra Adentro*, a WRTE (90.5 FM) radio program regarding the arts. Mercado's drawings have been published in *Luvina* and *Revista de la Universidad de Guadalajara*. She has exhibited her work at numerous venues, including the Riverside Arts Center (IL), the Oak Park Art League (IL), the México City Subway Station, the Cultural Center Mexiquense (Toluca, México), la Galería General de Justicia (México, D.F.), among many others.

Jennifer Morales lives in Milwaukee. She is an education policy researcher at the University of Wisconsin-Milwaukee and formerly worked for the anti-racist educational journal *Rethinking Schools*. She holds a B.A. in Modern Languages and Literatures from Beloit College. Morales' essay "Unpacking the White Privilege Diaper Bag" was published in *Everyday Acts Against Racism: Raising Children in a Multiracial World* (Seal Press, 1996).

Ana Ortiz de Montellano has lived in Northfield, Minnesota for over thirty years. She has taught writing at Carleton College, the Loft, SASE and elsewhere. She was Loft Mentor for emerging Latino writers in 1993 and won a Loft McKnight Award in Poetry in 1994. Her work has appeared in *Sing Heavenly Muse!, Sidewalks, Puerto del Sol*, and the anthologies *Latino Poetry, Two Worlds Walking,* and *Looking for Home: Women Writing about Exile*, among others.

Carmen Alicia Murguía is a native of Milwaukee and a community activist. She has participated in The Loft's Inroads Program for Emerging Hispanic/Chicano Writers, and in 1998 she received the Milwaukee County Arts Board "Art Futures" fellowship. Her poems, articles, editorials, and profiles have been published in *Zink, OUT Magazine, A.R.T.E Contar Historias, El Conquistador Latino News Source, The Spanish Journal, The Milwaukee Journal Sentinel, The Shepherd Express Metro, In Step Magazine,* and *The Wisconsin Light*, among others. In 1995 Murguía published her first collection of poetry *The Voices Inside: Mi Alma, Mi Cuerpo y Mi Espíritu.*

Beatriz Reid Dettloff lives in Milwaukee's Riverwest neighborhood and teaches at La Escuela Fratney, a two-way bilingual school. Her mother's family immigrated to San Francisco from México in 1920. Reid-Detloff has an M.A. in English from the University of Wisconsin-Madison. She published a chapbook *On This Earth* in 1999. Her poems have been included in the anthology *I Didn't Know There Were Latinos in Wisconsin*, and her "South Side Post Office Poem" was incorporated in Midwest Express Center, Milwaukee.

Graciela Reyes, born in Buenos Aires, teaches Pragmatic Linguistics at the University of Illinois at Chicago. She has published five poetry books, including *Poemas* (1991), *Que la quiero ver bailar* (1988), *Poemas para andar por casa* (1982), among others. Her most recent unpublished book is titled *Condiciones de felicidad*. Reyes' poems have also appeared in various anthologies and magazines published in Madrid, Barcelona, Buenos Aires, Montevideo and Chicago. She has won poetry contests in Spain and the U.S., among them the Letras de Oro Award from the University of Miami (1988). She has also published many short stories and articles regarding pedagogy. Reyes is currently working on a new collection of short stories.

Silvia Rivera Ramírez previously attended the University of Illinois at Chicago and is currently pursuing a B.A in Communications. She is a program producer at Radio Arte-WRTE, 90.5 FM, the youth-operated station where she hosts *Mexdiva,* a music show, and produces *Youth Metro,* a magazine-format talk program that explores social and cultural issues. Rivera also produced the CD *Scribbles Out Loud,* which contained four of her own poems, among a host of others by young authors at the Yollocalli Youth Museum.

Aidé Rodríguez received B.A. degrees in Sociology and History from the University of Michigan in 1999. While in Ann Arbor, she was an active participant in the A. Dinges and M. Lawrence Open-Mic Sessions and was featured in two accompanying collections, *Ascension* and *Libations*. She has participated in poetry readings in Ghana, West Africa, and at the Michigan Women of Color Conference. Rodríguez has written articles for *Reflejos*, a bilingual journal in West Dundee, Illinois. She currently works at the Mexican Fine Arts Center Museum in Chicago.

Nydia Rojas was born in Puerto Rico but now lives in Wisconsin. She is a bilingual resource specialist. Rojas' poetry and short stories have appeared in several magazines, among them *The Mad Poet Review, The Patterson Literary Review, Calyx, International Poetry Review*, and *The Wisconsin Academy Review*. In 1996, she won third place in the Chicano/Latino Literary Prize contest.

Irasema Salinas was born and raised in Chicago. She holds a B.A. in Journalism from Columbia College. Currently she is interning at *Chicago* Magazine. Salinas' poems have been published in *Piel Morena, Echo 2000-2001*, and at the <Poetry.com> web site.

Leda Schiavo was born in Argentina. She holds a Ph.D. and is a Professor of Spanish at the University of Illinois at Chicago. She has published a collection of poems entitled *Sin las debidas licencias / With Leave of License* and a volume of essays entitled *El éxtasis de los límites*.

Claudia Rosa Silva is of Mexican heritage. She grew up in the suburbs of Chicago but spent her childhood summers in San Luis Potosí. Silva holds an M.A. in History and B.A. degrees in Latin American Studies and Spanish from the University of Illinois. Her poetry has appeared in various Midwestern literary anthologies, such as the *Black and White* series from Outrider Press. Silva has performed her work at themed readings in the Chicagoland area.

Teresa Vázquez is an Afro-Cuban woman born and raised on the south side of Chicago. She has a B.A. in Creative Writing from Oberlin College and works as an Arts Administrator for the Association for the Advancement of Creative Musicians. Vázquez's particular interests lie in the performance of original spoken word and music that explore the continuums of sound and meaning. Several of her poems are recorded on her recently completed Audio Chapbook *A Woman Loving*. Other poems have been featured in *Womb Journeys: Beyond Regret, Joy and Shame* (Sun Crumbs, 2000). Vázquez is a member of the Livity Nyahbinghi Choir, a Chicago area Rastafarian drum and vocal ensemble.

About the Editors

Brenda Cárdenas holds an M.F.A. in Creative Writing from the University of Michigan-Ann Arbor. She has had poems published in *After Hours, RATTLE: Poetry for the 21st Century, Learning by Heart: Contemporary American Poetry About School, Under the Pomegranate Tree: The Best New Latino Erotica, Prairie Schooner, Tamaqua,* and others. Cárdenas received a 2000 Illinois Arts Council Finalist Award in Poetry. She has collaborated on several performance and conceptual art projects. Among them are *Oh Goya! Goya,* created with dancer/choreographer Evelyn Vélez Aguayo and performed at the Institute of Contemporary Arts in London, England, and *Undesirable Elements/Chicago* created by director Ping Chong with the cast members. She is currently writing and performing with *Sonido Ink(quieto),* a spoken word and music ensemble. Cárdenas has taught Latina/o Studies and writing courses at the University of Michigan, Wayne State University and the University of Illinois at Chicago. Presently, she teaches Creative Writing at the Yollocalli Youth Museum and WRTE-Radio Arte.

Johanny Vázquez Paz was born and raised in San Juan, Puerto Rico. She holds an M.A. in Hispanic Studies from the University of Illinois at Chicago and a B.A. in Sociology from Indiana State University. She has participated in poetry readings at various venues, such as The Chicago Cultural Center, Wheaton College, DePaul University, Columbia College, Notre Dame University, Indiana University and others. Her work has been included in the anthologies *Sin linderos ni arrabales, Hacia el Siglo XXI* (Part 1 and 2) and *Y Dios la hizo mujer!* (all published in Madrid, Spain) and has been published in the literary magazines *Beyond Borders* (DePaul Univ.), *Diminuendo* (Loyola Univ.), *Abrapalabra* (Univ. of Ill. at Chicago), *Karakola* (Chile), and *Yagrumal* (Puerto Rico). Vázquez Paz won the Voces Selectas 2000 poetry contest by Luz Bilingual Publishing (California) who, subsequently, published a selection of her poems in the collection *Carpetas de Luz.* She currently teaches Spanish at Olive Harvey College.

About MARCH/Abrazo Press

MARCH/Abrazo Press is an imprint of MARCH, Inc. (Movimiento Artístico Chicano), a not-for-profit cultural/arts organization incorporated in 1975. Its goal is to promote Chicana/o, Latina/o, and Native American Indian literary and visual arts expression with an emphasis on the Midwest by publishing perfect bound books and chapbooks. The books published over the past 19 years include Ken Serritos' *Saturn Calling*, Lonnie Poco's *Beside the Wichita*, Beatriz Badikian's *Akewa Is a Woman*, the anthology *Emergency Tacos: Seven Poets con Picante*, Carlos Cumpián's *Coyote Sun*, Raúl Niño's *Breathing Light*, Ed Two-Rivers' *A Dozen Cold Ones*, Raúl Rojas' and Marc Zimmerman's *Guatemala: Voces Desde el Silencio*, Trinidad Sanchez Jr.'s *Why Am I So Brown?*, Marc Zimmerman's *U.S. Latino Literature: An Essay and Annotated Bibliography*, Carlos Cortez Koyokuikatl's *de KANSAS a CALIFAS & back to CHICAGO*, Frank Varela's *Serpent Underfoot*, Mark Turcotte's *The Feathered Heart*, Olivia Maciel's *Más Salado Que Dulce/Saltier than Sweet*, and Michael Piazza's and Marc Zimmerman's *New World Disorders & Peripheral Strains: Cultural Dimensions in Latin American and Latino Studies*.

Permissions

"Am I Me?," "En esta Rica Costa No estamos en Costa Rica," "Reflections" by Denia Alvarado. Copyright © by Denia Alvarado, 2001. Used by permission of the author.

"Neither Here nor There," "I Have Been Painting on Leaves," "Our Work," "Cajas de zapatos / Shoeboxes" by Beatriz Badikian-Gartler. Copyright © by Beatriz Badikian-Gartler, 2001. Used by permission of the author.

"Container," "There Is Something" by Sonia Báez-Hernández. Copyright © by Sonia Báez-Hernández, 2001. Used by permission of the author.

"Spanish Sound Waves: Duración—*V*," "Spanish Sound Waves: Intensidad—*Ñ*," "Report from the Temple of Confessions in Old Chicano English" by Brenda Cárdenas. Copyright © by Brenda Cárdenas, 2001. Used by permission of the author. "Through Arms and Hands" by Brenda Cárdenas first appeared in *Floricanto: A Feast of the Arts 2000 Calendar*, published by Jeff Abbey Maldonado, 2000. Copyright © by Brenda Cárdenas, 2000. Reprinted by permission of the author.

"What Is Good Magic/Good Voodoo," "Nudity," "Because Blood Is Thinner" by Marta Collazo. Copyright © by Marta Collazo, 2001. Used by permission of the author.

"Guerra" / "War," "Political Exiles," "Past" by Daisy Cubias. Copyright © by Daisy Cubias, 2001. Used by permission of the author.

"Auf Zweifel / To Doubt," "Call," "Iguazú," "Aullando" / "Howling," "Oigo el pasar de la vida" / "I Hear the Passing of Life" by Silvia Divinetz. Copyright © by Silvia Divinetz, 2001. Used by permission of the author. "Howling" by Silvia Divinetz first appeared in *Nimrod,* Vol. 41, No. 2, Spring/Summer, 1998. Copyright © by Silvia Divinetz, 1998. Reprinted by permission of the author.

"Cebollas," "Hermanita, Hermanota," "Pinki" by Venessa Maria Fuentes. Copyright © by Venessa Maria Fuentes, 2001. Used by permission of the author. "Birthday" by Venessa Maria Fuentes first appeared in *Swerve,* Vol. 1, Issue 1. Copyright © by Venessa Maria Fuentes, 1999. Reprinted by permission of the author.